Nightwork

Nightwork

A History of Hacks and Pranks at MIT

Institute Historian T. F. Peterson

Published in association with the MIT Museum

The MIT Press
Cambridge, Massachusetts
London, England

This book was set in Bembo and Stone sans serif by the MIT Press.
Printed and bound in the United States of America.

Library of Congress Cataloging-in-Publication Data

Peterson, T. F.
Nightwork : a history of hacks and pranks at MIT / T.F. Peterson
p. cm.
"Published in association with the MIT Museum."
ISBN 0-262-66137-3 (pbk. : alk. paper)
1. Massachusetts Institute of Technology—History. 2. Student activities—Massachusetts—Cambridge—History. 3. College students—Massachusetts—Cambridge—Humor. 4. College wit and humor. I. MIT Museum. II. Title.
T171.M49 P48 2003
378.744'4—dc21

2002035753

10 9 8 7 6 5 4 3 2

Contents

Foreword

Jane Pickering, Director, MIT Museum

MIT Museum's extensive collections include historic artifacts significant in the life of the Institute: slide rules, computers, molecular models, a police car. A police car? Well, the shell of a police car. Along with giant scrubbing bubbles, buzzword bingo cards, and a gargantuan Jolt Cola can, that old Chevy carcass is part of one of our most beloved collections—MIT hacks.

On my arrival at MIT, I quickly realized that the Museum's previous two books about hacks at MIT were required reading. I also found that this collection of objects, letters, photos, and newsclippings presented unique problems for a museum. How do we preserve objects designed for a lifetime that is measured in hours rather than years? How do we predict which hacks will be part of Institute folklore in fifty years and which will be forgotten? For that matter, how do we decide whether something is a hack or not? After several meetings with MIT graduates and other interested parties, we developed guidelines for collecting hacks. I began to understand the place of these events at MIT, and, like everybody else in the community, eagerly awaited each new hack.

Working on this book has been one of my most entertaining tasks as museum director, mostly because of the group of people we recruited to work with us. Kathy Thurston-Lighty, our writer and editor, has produced this wonderful (and incredibly detailed!) text, and collections assistant Jenny O'Neill worked miracles organizing the large number of photographs. Andrew Chen ('96) helped with photo scanning. The editorial committee—Erin Conwell ('03), Edmund Golaski ('99), André DeHon ('91), and Terri Iuzzolino Matsakis ('93)—provided information, guidance, and links to the community. They profess, however, having no practical experience with hacks themselves. Terri, in particular, is a longtime friend of the Museum and has acted as our volunteer hacks archivist for many years. Finally, many thanks go to the Peter de Florez Fund for Humor at MIT for providing the support necessary to make this book a reality.

Introduction

Institute Historian T. F. Peterson

In 1914, MIT chose the beaver as its mascot from the pages of *Mr. Hornaday's Book on the Animals of North America.* Lester Gardner (class of 1898) explained why its candidacy was uncontested: "Of all the animals in the world," he said, reading straight from Hornaday, "the beaver is noted for his engineering and mechanical skills and habits of industry. [He is] nocturnal, he does his best work in the dark."

Regardless of superficial changes to the campus culture, such as the introduction of computers, the MIT animal has remained true to Hornaday's description at the turn of the twentieth century. The MIT student eats, thinks, daydreams, and socializes under the light of the silvery moon. The black canvas of night is the stimulus for invention. And thus most of the work of hacking—the brainstorming, the strategy sessions, the prep, the test runs, the implementation—happen at night. They may be unveiled by the light of day, but more often than not, they are created by night.

Of course, MIT hackers also emulate the sheer ingenuity of the school mascot. An MIT hack, like science and technology itself, is judged by how elegantly it accomplishes its objective. The hacking hat trick at the 1982 Harvard-Yale football game, for example, was to many hacking connoisseurs quintessential in its elegance (see When MIT Won the Harvard-Yale Game). It reflected the preparation, efficiency, and whimsy that all the most venerable hacks display. More than that, it was a charmingly self-aware, even self-deprecatory statement—another characteristic of the most effective hacks. It said, "Sure, it may be laughable that we could win a football game by our athletic prowess, but we definitely can win it with our brains." And although they took home no trophies, win they did—with an enormous black MIT balloon at the 46-yard line.

In the twenty years since the balloon burst from the turf of Harvard Stadium, hacking has matured along with the wider culture. When the fraternity responsible for the Harvard-Yale Game hack later admitted its role in the prank, it broke a cardinal rule of hacking culture, a rule that is far more stringently observed today: hacking is about stealth, not self-aggrandizement.

It's about quiet determination, not unlike that of a certain modest but enterprising woodland animal.

The standards of contemporary hacking etiquette decree that it is also uncouth to create a hack that leaves so much as a disfiguring mark on its environment, and certainly the hack disturbed a bit of turf at the Harvard-Yale game. By the mid-nineties, the challenge of pulling off a great hack included sensitivity to environmental impact. Although the 1994 Entertainment and Hacking frieze required the Institute's Confined Space Rescue Team to rappel down a sheer wall to remove the hack, the CSRT did so with the help of step-by-step dismantling instructions that the hackers delivered to campus authorities.

Irregularities of etiquette aside, the Harvard-Yale Game hack exemplifies a key tenet of the sport: the success of a hack is almost directly proportionate to the strength of its finer points. And few hacks have been as successful as the legendary Campus Police Car on the Dome hack (see Domework). Passersby began to notice it as dawn broke, but many campus authorities first heard about the hack on the metro-Boston traffic reports. Positioned on the dome, as if atop a grand auto showroom dais, sat the metal shell of a Chevy Cavalier painted to look like a campus police car, its roof lights flashing. A dummy dressed as a police officer sat behind the wheel with a half-eaten box of donuts. The car was number π and bore a parking ticket with the offense "no permit for this location."

The Campus Police Car hack is a striking example of how pranks at MIT differ from those at other schools. As Jay Keyser points out in his thought-provoking essay about the drive to hack, MIT students typically don't dress statues of founding fathers in ladies underwear (see Where the Sun Shines, There Hack They). They make large objects appear in inaccessible places, rewire lecture hall blackboards, or place a police car or a working telephone booth atop the dome. "They make fun of engineering," Keyser says, "by impersonating it and then pulling the seat out from under."

But Keyser, as you will read, would be the last to dismiss hacking as a frivolous manifestation of the Institute's engineering culture. For some MIT students, hacking is part and parcel of an MIT education. It teaches them to work productively in teams, to solve engineering problems, and to communicate to the wider world. André DeHon ('91), discusses how hacking reflects the Institute's own value system (see Mastery over the Physical World). "Hacks provide an opportunity to demonstrate creativity and know-how in mastering the physical world," DeHon observes. "At MIT, intellect and its application are valued and not, for example, athletic prowess. It's not that we can run faster than you can. It's that we can manipulate the physical world to do things you hadn't imagined were possible." Is this the real reason a beaver builds a dam—because he can? Surely it is something that the other animals of the forest cannot pull off.

This book pursues the culture of hacking from a myriad of angles, not unlike how hackers work. It explores hacking through the physical aspects and the psychological aspects, through the broad statements and the finer details. The book also examines the evolution of hacking as a sport and includes first-hand accounts and thoughtful ruminations from students and faculty about hacking. For the uninitiated, a glossary explains insider terminology like "Rush" and "IAP" and explores the meaning of the word *hack*.

Herewith, I set you loose onto the playing fields of hackdom.

Where No Cow Has Gone Before: Accessing the Inaccessible

Armchair aficionados of the sport often assume that hacking was a twentieth-century phenomenon. But even before the Institute crossed the bridge from Boston to Cambridge in 1916, MIT students were hacking. John Ripley Freeman, renowned civil engineer and member of the class of 1875, noted in his memoirs that pranksters habitually sprinkled iodide of nitrogen, a mild contact explosive, on the drill room floor, adding considerable snap to routine assembly.

Of course, pranksters weren't called hackers back then; only within the last thirty years has the term hack been synonymous with campus hijinks (see Hack, Hacker, Hacking). But it was in those formative years of hacking at MIT—well before the term was coined—that the spirit and traditions of the sport were established.

Institute hacks in the late nineteenth and early twentieth centuries were primitive by today's standards—jokes played on professors or pranks sparked by inter-class rivalries. Freshmen would steal the sophomore class flag before the annual football game. Sophomores would rearrange the furniture in freshmen dorm rooms while students were at class meetings. But in the 1920s, the Dorm Goblin, the first documented hacking group, raised the bar, setting the standard for subsequent generations of MIT hackers to follow or surpass.

In January 1928, the Dorm Goblin threaded a 35-foot telegraph pole through Senior House Dormitory and a few months later coaxed a live cow to the roof of the '93 dorm. (She went up fairly happily but was none too pleased to make the trip down.) This early "cow prank" set a trend that inspired the title of Neil Steinberg's book about college pranks, *If At All Possible, Involve a Cow* (St. Martin's, 1992). The addition of social responsibility to the hackers' creed in the late twentieth century made them revert to fiberglass bovinus (see Dome as Dais).

The Dorm Goblin moved on to more technical pranks, like turning dormitory phones into radio speakers, which allowed students to fill their rooms with the latest tunes by taking the receiver off the hook. The Goblin was also more than likely responsible for launching the door hacking tradition that persisted for decades (see Door Man).

Since the earliest days of the Dorm Goblin, one underlying motivation behind MIT pranks has been to conquer the inaccessible and make possible the improbable. Often hackers have employed this vision in the creation of surrealist still lifes or absurd dioramas—a telephone booth on top of one of the Institute's signature domes, for example, or a dormitory room set up on the frozen Charles River. Full-size sailboats have found their way into moats and swimming pools.

But making possible the improbable requires skill, attention to detail, and careful research. In 1976, for example, hackers consulted an arachnologist and examined spider webs with an electron microscope before constructing the multi-storied Burton Spider Web with 1,250 feet of nylon rope and steel wire.

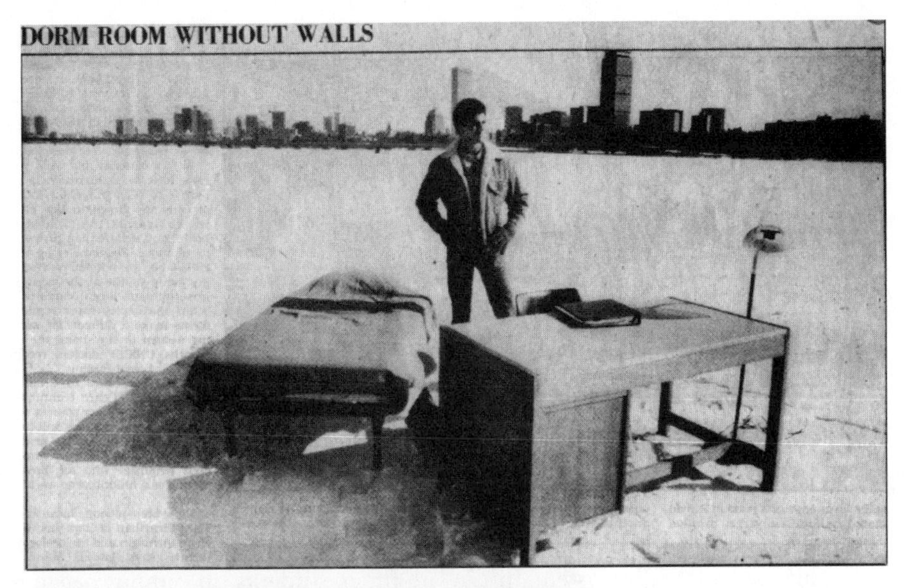
DORM ROOM WITHOUT WALLS

Hack, Hacker, Hacking

Brian Leibowitz

The fifties saw the beginnings of the MIT term hack. The origin of the term in the MIT slang is elusive—different meanings have come in and out of use, and it was rarely used in print before the 1970s. Furthermore, the use of hack varied among different groups of students at MIT. "Hacking" was used by many MIT students to describe any activity undertaken to avoid studying—this could include goofing off, playing bridge, talking to friends, or going out. Performing pranks was also called hacking, but only as part of the broader definition. In the middle to late fifties, additional meanings for the word hack were developed by members of the Tech Model Railroad Club, including an article or project without constructive end or an unusual and original solution to a problem, such as inventing a new circuit for a switching system. In the late fifties, students on campus began to use the word as a noun to describe a prank.

Also in the late fifties, telephone hacking, the study of the internal codes and features of telephone switching systems, emerged. Here, the word hack was used to imply doing something outside the norm; telephone systems were made to do things that the system designers never anticipated.

In the late sixties and the seventies, the meaning of the word hack broadened to include activities that tested limits of skill, imagination, and wits. Hacking was investigating a subject for its own sake and not for academic advancement, exploring the inaccessible places on campus, doing something clandestine or out of the ordinary, and performing pranks.

The word hack found its way into common usage outside MIT with the advent of computer hacking in the early sixties. In the eighties, experts in the computer field made a distinction between hacking and cracking. Hacking denotes nondestructive mischief while cracking describes activities such as unleashing a computer virus, breaking into a computer, or destroying data.

By the mid eighties, hacking had come to be used at MIT primarily to describe pranks and exploring the Institute. Many of the earlier definitions have disappeared from use on campus.

Auto Industry: The Great Vehicle Hacks

Hackers celebrated the mass production of the automobile by adopting it as the prop of choice. During the 1920s and 1930s, MIT pranksters hauled cars up the sides of dormitories, parked them on the front steps of buildings, and even impaled a Ford coupe on a steel pole.

In January 1926 the Dorm Goblin hauled a Ford chassis, with engine intact, up five stories to the roof of the '93 dormitory (now the East Campus dormitory) and perched the front wheels rakishly over the side. According to myth, the triumphant student pictured in the driver's seat was none other than James Killian, class of 1926, Institute president from 1949 to 1959, and Killian Court namesake. Students again pulled a car up the side of the building in 1936.

On another occasion the Dorm Goblin surreptitiously, and with nary a scratch to the vehicle, moved an illegally parked touring car to the basement of the '93 dormitory. The removal required a team of sixteen workers and a tractor. In 1959, in tribute to an identical hack nearly thirty years earlier, hackers parked a car on the top step of the steep flight up to the Walker Memorial building.

Cars took a back seat to other props until the latter years of the twentieth century, when hackers jump-started the tradition of vehicle hacks in 1985 with the artful placement of a VW beetle at the entrance to the Zeta Beta Tau fraternity. The Bug's nose jutted out over the front steps as though it had just burst out of the frat house after a wild ride.

As it turned out, 1985 was a particularly rich year for vehicle hacks. In that same year, hackers created the legendary "Massachusetts Toolpike" hack. ("Tool" is an MIT expression for studying, and the Massachusetts Turnpike is a major interstate heading west out of Cambridge.) The Toolpike encompassed the entire central thoroughfare of the Institute. In Lobby 7, MIT's main foyer, hackers hung a sign: "Massachusetts Toolpike: Toll $16,000" (a year's tuition at the time). They created angled parking spaces in the building and neatly parked an actual car in one. With yellow tape, they divided the 775-foot "Infinite Corridor" into lanes complete with a rotary. Along the "Toolpike," they posted highway signs instructing travelers about regulations and tolls, such as "SPEED LIMIT 3×10^{10} cgs." At the Toolpike's terminus at 77 Massachusetts Avenue, the final sign read: "Exit 77 Real World."

This vehicle hack remained unsurpassed for nearly a decade until hackers mounted one of the finest hacks of all time—the Campus Police Car on the Dome. But hacks on the dome fall into a category all to themselves....

SPEED
LIMIT
3×10
10
(cgs)

CHRIS
JACK
JENS
BILL
Francesco
JIM
Bryan
WARREN
Class of 1989
MASSACHVSETTS TOOLPIKE
TOLL $16,000
SCHUMANN
Symphony #3
PROKOFIEV
Concerto #3
Saturday
Dec 14
8:30
KRESGE
CURRENT INFORMATION

RICHARD

Hacking Ethics

The irreverent HowToGAMIT Guide *(How to Get around MIT) is the ultimate MIT handbook. This excerpt from* HowToGAMIT *sets forth the hackers' code as it stands in the early twenty-first century.*

1. Be *safe.* Your safety, the safety of your fellow hackers, and the safety of anyone you hack should never be compromised.

2. Be *subtle.* Leave no evidence that you were ever there.

3. Leave things as you found them (or better).

4. If you find something broken call F-IXIT (the local number for reporting problems with the buildings and grounds). Hackers often go places that Institute workers do not frequent regularly and may see problems before anyone else.

5. Leave no damage.

6. Do not steal anything.

7. Brute force is the last resort of the incompetent. ("One who breaks a thing to find out what it is has left the path of reason."—*Keshlam the Seer, Knight of the Random Order*)

8. Do not hack while under the influence of alcohol/drugs/etc.

9. Do not drop things (off a building) without a ground crew.

10. Do not hack alone (just like swimming).

11. Above all, exercise *common sense.*

Domework: Hacking the Domes

The Institute's two signature domes have always been popular venues for hackers' surrealist dioramas. The smaller of the massive spheres is 72 feet in diameter and 100 feet high. The Great Dome measures 108 feet in diameter and 150 feet high. At the top of each dome is a flat platform approximately 20 feet in diameter. The appearance of a cow, a prosthetic device, or a dorm room is all the more dramatic because each of these two platforms is accessible only through a small hatch. A good deal of the art of a dome hack is the elegance of the solution hackers find to overcome that challenge.

In the predawn hours of May 9, 1994, early-rising students were drawn to lights flashing on the dome. As the sky lightened, the whir of traffic helicopters alerted other students and staff. Campus Police Chief Anne Glavin heard about the situation on the news while driving to work. Nuance by nuance, the day unveiled the legendary Campus Police Car on the Dome hack.

The luminous spring sky proved an ideal backdrop against which to view the white car glinting in the sun 150 feet above the ground on the grand dais of MIT's Great Dome. The bar of emergency lights across the police car's roof flashed with mock urgency, and the car appeared to contain an acrophobic campus police officer frozen with fear in the driver's seat.

As with most of the great hacks, this installation was both more and less than it appeared to be. Those on the ground could not see, for example, that the dummy police officer was cooling her heels behind the wheel with a toy gun, a cup of coffee, and a box of donuts. Neither from the ground nor from the air could spectators appreciate the details: fuzzy dice hanging from the rear-view mirror, a yellow sign on the back window warning "I Break for Donuts," a parking ticket affixed to the windshield saying "No permit for this location," the IHTFP license plate, or the car number being π. But details, seen or unseen, are a point of honor with hackers.

Because it was painted authentically, spectators also could not detect that this MIT Campus Police car was no more than a bit of stage set. Hackers had attached segments of the outer metal shell of a Chevrolet Cavalier to sections of wooden framing making it possible for them to fit each piece through the 3' × 4' hatch that leads to the dome and then assemble the vehicle on site.

By 10 on the morning of its unveiling, physical plant workers had removed the hack, but news of the event proliferated. The story hit the evening news and the wire services spread it worldwide. At the campus movie that evening, the ads that ran before the previews included this appeal: "Missing: One white and blue patrol car. If found, call x3-1212."

Dome as Dais

The engineering challenge and the dramatic possibilities make MIT's domes two favorite hacking venues. Here are a few of the most legendary dome hacks:

Centennial Hack, 1961

To celebrate the Institute's one hundredth birthday, a group of first-year students place a nine-foot cardboard candle on the Great Dome along with a happy birthday banner.

Great Pumpkin, 1962 and 1994

On Halloween night in 1962, hackers transform the Great Dome into a smiling jack-o-lantern. In 1992, a professional construction crew working on the renovation of the MIT Press Bookstore building pays homage to the original Great Pumpkin hack by creating its own jack-o-lantern on the orange mesh surrounding the building. Hackers continue the tradition by mounting yet another on the Great Dome in 1994.

Kilroy Is Here, 1972

In an amazing feat of "textile engineering," hackers celebrate Halloween by recreating the World War II icon with 6,000 square feet of polyethylene sheeting.

The Big Screw, 1977 and 1985

The screw is a recurring motif in the social history of the Institute. Every year, the APO fraternity bestows the "Institute Screw Award" upon the individual deemed to have been the most successful at "screwing" MIT students. It is thus inevitable that both large and small domes are eventually "screwed."

The Great Breast of Knowledge, 1979

A hacking group by the name of the Burton One Outdoor Breast Society finally accomplishes its objective to adorn the dome with the nipple that has been conspicuous by its absence for three quarters of a century (see The Great Breast of Knowledge).

Steer on the Dome, 1979

On Halloween, hackers "rescue" a life-sized fiberglass steer from its grassy knoll in front of the Hilltop Steakhouse and give it a more prominent grazing field on the Great Dome. When "Ferdi" is returned, the Hilltop management places a mortar board on its head and a diploma in its mouth.

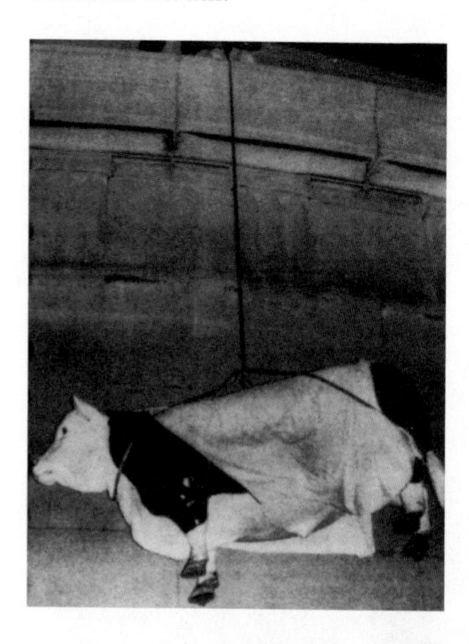

Phone on the Dome, 1982

When the campus policeman scales the dome to investigate, he realizes that the telephone booth is indeed the real thing. In fact, the booth light is on and the phone is ringing.

Home on the Dome, 1986

To alleviate crowding in the dormitories, the Technology Hackers Association constructs a 12-foot-high, 16-foot-square house, complete with mailbox and welcome mat. The twenty-eight panels of Room 10-1000 are hauled up the side of the building and secured with ropes and cables.

Snowman, 1987 and 2001

On a steamy August day in 1987, hackers erect a papier-mâché snowman on the small dome. In 2001, they build one actually made of snow.

Holiday Lights, 1990 and 1993

Hackers spell out "MIT" with Christmas lights on the small dome in 1990 and then illuminate the same dome with an 8 × 10-foot menorah for Chanukah in 1993.

Witch's Hat, 1993

In recognition of Halloween, hackers construct what is purported to be the world's largest witch's hat on the small dome. Approximately 20-feet tall and supported by a 15-foot-wide brim, the hat weathers a very windy weekend before its removal on Monday morning—a tribute to the engineering skills of the hacking team.

Contents under Pressure, 1993 and 2001

In 1993, hackers transform the small dome into a giant pressure cooker with a massive dial and a banner that reads "Warning: Contents Vnder Pressvre!" In 2001, another symbol of stress appears during finals—this time, on the Great Dome. To the naked eye, the MIT landmark looks to have cracked under the weight of an 8-foot-tall "48-unit" weight—forty-eight being the number of units in the standard MIT course load. Carefully secured with cables, the "Acme" weight is accompanied by a long strip of fabric representing the crack.

Campus Police Car, 1994

As the sun rises on a fine spring day in May, traffic helicopters begin to report a police car parked on the Great Dome (see Domework).

Beanie Cap, 1996

With strategically placed red stripes alternating against the gray of the dome, and a spinning propeller on top, hackers transform the Great Dome into a fully-functioning propeller beanie. They round out the prank with a second hack on the Institute's official "Hackbusters" vehicle (see It's Not a Job, It's an Adventure).

Cheesehead, 1997

When the Green Bay Packers, a.k.a. the "Cheeseheads," win over the New England Patriots in the Super Bowl, hackers place a giant chunk of faux cheese on the Great Dome.

Great Droid, 1999

Two days before the much-awaited *Phantom Menace* installment of the *Star Wars* movie series, hackers turn the Great Dome into the Great Droid. R2-D2 is recreated in authentic color using fabric panels and a painted tent to represent the droid's holographic projector. Hackers thoughtfully include detailed disassembly instructions addressed to the "Imperial Drones" and signed "Rebel Scum."

The Eagle Has Landed, 1999

On the thirtieth anniversary of the first moon landing, hackers create a man-on-the-moon diorama on the small dome. MIT alumnus Edwin E. "Buzz" Aldrin Jr., Sc.D., was the second person to walk on the moon.

Ring around the Dome, 2001

In anticipation of the release of the first *Lord of the Rings* movie, a gold ring with red Elvish script appears around the Great Dome. The ring is authentically inscribed with Tolkein's text, about which Gandalf remarked, "The letters are Elvish, of an ancient mode, but the language is that of Mordor, which I will not utter here." The official MIT hacking website, the IHTFP gallery, notes that hackers were "not completely successful, for neither the Great Dome nor Building 10 vanished into the realm of the shadows."

Greener Pastures: The Green Building Hacks

MIT's Green Building is a hacker's dream. It's tall—the tallest building on campus, rising 23 stories to 277 feet. It has ample display space—a symmetrical grid of more than 150 windows. It's highly visible—from both Boston and Cambridge. It even has its own dome—a massive radar dome (or radome) that sits atop the flat roof. Not surprisingly, even before construction was finished in 1964, hackers had already staked their claim by suspending a "Tech is Hell" banner from the highest tip of the pile driver parked at the site.

Over the years, hackers have employed the Green Building's 26.5-foot radome as a sort of mannequin. In 1983 they fashioned it into a smiley face using giant yellow building tarps. In 2001, they turned the dome into a "Magic Pi Ball" in honor of spring finals. A spoof on the "Magic Eight Ball," a perennially popular toy for predicting the future, the Magic Pi gave a quintessential "eight ball" response to students who sought exam advice: "Outlook hazy. Try again."

Because of its visibility from the Charles River Esplanade, hackers have often mounted Green Building hacks to entertain the enormous crowds that line the banks for the annual concert and fireworks on Independence Day. In 1986, when the Boston Pops was lured to New York City to celebrate the rededication of the Statue of Liberty, Bostonians were left without their traditional concert on the Esplanade. Hackers resolved that a trade was in order—the Pops for the statue. They transformed the radar dome into Lady Liberty herself standing watch from her high perch over the Esplanade.

The idea was simple, the execution not so. Hackers arrived on site with an extension ladder so as to reach the hatch on the radar dome but quickly realized the ladder would not fit in the elevator, nor up the stairs. Luckily, the team had brought along 300 feet of rope...just in case. Using the rope, they hauled the ladder up the side of the building; a hacker wearing a safety harness then mounted the radome and guided the network of spikes around the lightning rod. The crown was actually constructed of aluminum masts sheathed in white cloth and mounted on a wooden base, its underside lined with carpeting to protect the radar dome. Guy wires kept it in place. With the

artful positioning of a yellow sheet, the crow's nest that rises beside the radar dome was pressed into service as Liberty's torch. Thus, a sense of civic balance was achieved as the Pops serenaded New York.

A few years later, on July 4, 1993, hackers turned the building into the "World's Largest Sound Meter." Hackers converted the ventilation ducts across the top of the Green Building into a VU (sound) meter. Created from 6 × 4 foot apertures that were illuminated by bright red lights, the 5000+ watt meter was, at 250 times the size of an ordinary stereo sound meter, the largest in the world. The light show was keyed to the music of the Pops concert, and later to the sounds of the fireworks. The delighted crowd watched as "Cylon" scanning light patterns (reminiscent of *Battlestar Galactica*) alternated with one-dimensional Tetris and even "IHTFP" in Morse code.

Greenspeak Spoken Here

To MIT hackers, one of the Green Building's most inspiring characteristics is its fenestration, which they have turned, time after time, into an enormous message board. In the Institute vernacular, this genre of hacks has come to be known as *Greenspeak*—the art of turning on and off lights and raising and lowering window shades to broadcast a message.

The first recorded instance of Greenspeak occurred in March 1964—before the Green Building was even completed. The Theta Chi fraternity used the medium to increase their visibility, pulling off a giant "θX." Not to be outdone, the venerable hacking group "Jack Florey" used Greenspeak the next day to flash that iconic acronym of MIT life, IHTFP (see Intriguing Hacks to Fascinate People).

Over the years, hackers have used Greenspeak to celebrate life's big moments. Some of the most attention-getting:

Moonwalk, 1969

When the Apollo 11 mission delivers Neil Armstrong and Edwin "Buzz" Aldrin ('63) to the moon's surface, hackers celebrate in Greenspeak, displaying a towering number 11 across the Green Building facade.

Holiday Lights, 1973 and 1975

Hackers create a Christmas tree in Greenspeak, and two years later a jack-o-lantern for Halloween.

East Campus Pointer, 1979 through the present

With a simple but attention-getting "EC→" The East Campus dormitory periodically uses Greenspeak to attract first-year students during residential recruitment.

Red Sox vs. Mets, 1986

Hackers have to add diplomacy to the usual kit bag of skills when Mets fans initially refuse to pull down their window shades nearly thwarting attempts to spell out "SOX" during the 1986 World Series. Ultimately the New York fans have their way, Greenspeaking "2" when the Mets prevail over the Red Sox.

Good Will Hunting, 1998

On Oscar® night, hackers span the fenestration to recreate the golden statuette in recognition of the Academy Awards® bestowed for *Good Will Hunting*, a film set at MIT.

Intriguing Hacks to Fascinate People

The origins of the acronym IHTFP are strictly anecdotal. Many have claimed the amorphous motto as their own. Its use has been unofficially documented in both the United States Air Force and at MIT as far back as the 1950s. Whatever its ancestry, generations of MIT students have delighted in the acronym's infinite versatility. "IHTFP" has appeared on sign posts and in Greenspeak; it's even been printed on shoelaces. The point is to use it creatively: I Hate to Face Physics, It's Hard to Fondle Penguins, I Have Truly Found Paradise. And of course there's the age-old tuition gripe, I Have to Forever Pay. But these flights of fancy are merely riffs on IHTFP's widely accepted primary meaning: "I Hate This F*&^ing Place."

MCMXVI
INSTITVTE OF

Crash
ASSACHVSETTS·INST

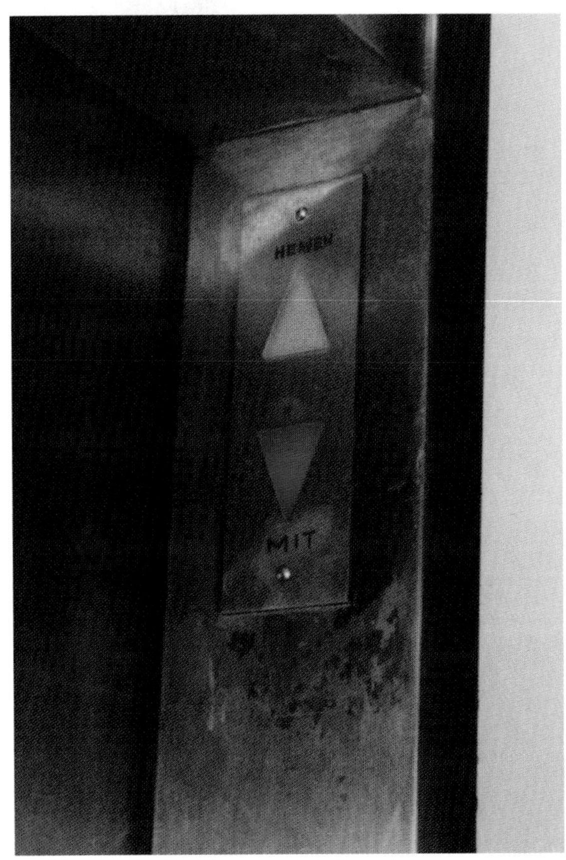
MIT

GO
SLOW
GEEKS CROSSI
AHEAD

0.8-THOU SHALT NOT EXCEED
THE SPEED OF LIGHT
0.9-KEEP HOLY THE MONTH
OF IAP FOR IT IS A
TIME OF REST.
0.A-IHTFP.
0.B-THOU SHALT NOT SLEEP.
0.C-THOU SHALT CONSUME CAFFEINE.
0.D-THOU SHALT NOT TAKE
PASS/FAIL IN VAIN.
0.E-THOU SHALT NOT COVET THY
NEIGHBOR'S HP.
0.F-THOU SHALT NOT DIVIDE BY ZERO.

Making an Entrance: The Lobby 7 Hacks

It stands to reason that Lobby 7, the heavily-trafficked main foyer to the campus, would be a popular venue for grand-scale hacks and, over the years, it has inspired pranks that live large in Institute lore. Generations of students have passed through this gateway only to be greeted by welcome mats of bubblewrap, an enormous rope swing, an intricate maze, a giant chess board, and on the prominent stone pedestals that frame the lobby, a student dressed as a military memorial on one occasion, and on another, Winnie the Pooh.

In 1986, when graduate students in the architecture department's Building Technology Group suspended a space station prototype in Lobby 7, the Order of Random Knights hacking group wrapped it in 1,600 square feet of cloth, turning it into a massive six-sided die. In 2001, hackers created a faux archaeological excavation site for the unearthing of a "large black monolith." They erected barriers and posted an authentic-looking sign showing a man in a chemical hazard suit digging up a massive black rectangle. An allusion to 2001: A Space Odyssey, the large black monolith was the star of more than one hack during the lifespan of the Class of 2001.

The hacks in Lobby 7 have ranged from the whimsically absurd—a downpour of 1,600 pink and green ping pong balls—to the monumentally surreal—a full-service cathedral complete with stained glass windows, organ, and a wedding ceremony. A couple legally tied the knot during this 1992 hack, appropriately titled "Cathedral of Our Lady of the All-Night Tool." It is the only hack on record that enjoys that distinction.

Given the sheer breadth and depth of the "Cathedral" event, which took place on the eve of Halloween, it is not surprising that a team of approximately sixty people carried out this hack, which sources say had been on the drawing board since June. In addition to the intricate stained glass windows, mahogany pews, and massive stone tablets presenting the commandments, the hack included a computerized confessional manned by Father Eliza, who ran on an Apple II+ and had to be rebooted when sins overwhelmed (see Father Tool's Grand Tour).

VLTVRE AND COMMERC

CLARK ABT
7 pm
8:00
SATURDAY
9:00
front of
athletic
center

The Cathedral was actually a sequel to a 1990 performance hack during which hackers from ORK dressed as monks and marched across campus chanting "Oh My God, Do We Need Sleep!" in Latin while handing out flyers for Our Lady of the All-Night Tool. Other hacks followed suit—the 1994 Beer Shrine hack, for example, which turned Lobby 7 into an elaborate rathskeller complete with Beer Commandments, diagrams on brewing beer, and a towering arched shrine constructed entirely of beer cans.

Conveniently enough, Lobby 7 is located directly under the small dome. The inside of the dome and the delicate skylight at its pinnacle are as challengingly inaccessible as the exterior of the dome—the only difference being that the challenge is concave rather than convex. Hackers have overcome the obstacle of this 90-foot-high vaulted space to present all manner of artifacts and symbols. They have suspended an enormous disco ball, an elaborate spider web, and a lighted jack-o-lantern. They've used the skylight to illuminate smiley faces, the Jurassic Park symbol, and Batman's official crest.

Two of the most ingenious hacks in the history of hackdom were executed on the inscription that rings the bottom edge of the dome at the fourth floor level. In August of 1994, hackers greeted incoming students with a bold, if subtle, welcome banner. They replaced the institutional slogan engraved in stone with one of their own.

What once read…

Established for Advancement and Development of Science its Application to Industry the Arts Agriculture and Commerce. Charter MDCCCLXI

now proclaimed…

Established for Advancement and Development of Science its Application to Industry the Arts *Entertainment and Hacking.* Charter MDCCCLXI.

The edit was accomplished with Styrofoam panels faux finished to blend with the rest of the inscription and was held in place by virtually imperceptible spring-loaded braces. The modification was so subtle, in fact, that campus

ARTS

police officers called to the scene to investigate suspicious activity found nothing out of the ordinary on their first two trips. Students and staff, learning of the hack, stared in puzzlement trying to figure out what had changed in the inscription. When finally they were able to distinguish the hacked panels from the original, the newly-formed Confined Space Rescue Team (see It's Not a Job, It's an Adventure) rappelled down into Lobby Seven to remove it, determining that such a maneuver was the only way the hack could have been installed.

Three years later, celebrating Halloween 1997, hackers pulled off another stunning alteration of the Lobby 7 architecture, perching four enormous gargoyles on a ledge beneath the dome. Although fashioned of papier-mâché from hundreds of copies of a free newspaper distributed on campus, the six-foot-tall statues gazed down onto Lobby 7 with eerie authority and authentic grotesquerie. Passersby who had never had cause to look up, assumed they were stone statues original to the building. Closer inspection revealed, however, that one figure bore a striking resemblance to Dilbert and another to a beaver, the school mascot.

ARTS

Father Tool's Grand Tour

Brothers and Sisters,

Let us take a guided tour of Cathedral Seven, the Cathedral of Our Lady of the All-Night Tool.

The first thing we notice is the striking stained-glass window that occupies the rear wall of our cathedral (west side, 77 Mass. Ave. entrance). It is composed of three distinct panels. The leftmost (as viewed from inside the Cathedral) depicts a common scene in the life of the devout tool—an MIT lecture hall, complete with students, blackboards, and professor. The center contains a rosette featuring the animal that walks most closely to the father above—a beaver (Brass Rat style). The rightmost panel shows the Killian Court view of the Institute, complete with Dome and a representative Tool—note that the Tool stands on top of a large stack of unmarked bills in order to gain entrance to the 'tute. The stained-glass window is quite striking when viewed from the side with the least light (inside during the day, outside at night). Also, when the father above sends us sunlight without clouds, the light shines through the glass and makes soft, clear images on the pillars (east side).

Looking skyward, we see that the formerly-dull skylight now radiates with light and color. In the central circle resides the logo of the goddess dear to many, an Athena Owl. Radiating outward from the center are pie-shaped wedges. There are sixteen in all, colored alternately purple and blue. In each wedge is housed one of the many truths which forms the foundation of our faith.

Of course, you all hear the inspirational music produced by our lovely organ. The present verse repeats hourly for all to enjoy. It starts with Bach's "Toccata and Fugue in D Minor" and continues with many inspiring pieces including some Gregorian chants. We can see the organ that produces this wonderful music on the second floor balcony (second floor, center east, directly at end of second-floor Infinite Corridor). Notice the ornate gold and silver pipes tuned for musical perfection. To take a closer look, we venture to the second floor. Here, we see the light from the middle window (Beaver) shines nicely onto the organ. The keyboard is constructed from six computer keyboards (four VT-100 and two which are believed to be of the Knight-TV system style). A close look at the keyboards reveals that important messages are contained within them as well (Nerd Pride, 37619*, IHTFP, Our Lady of the All Night Tool, 3.14159).

神愛世人

Returning to the ground level, we note the row of pews on the south side of the Cathedral, facing east and the altar. The pews look quite like they belong in this Cathedral and it bemuses everyone. Few actually realize that the "pews" have always been in Lobby 7. A historical note—when originally installed, a different set of "pews" were used. The original set resembled lecture-hall seats. The pews were upgraded to their current status when a need elsewhere for the original pews became apparent. The altar has a "marble" top and has vintage 1971 4K core memory inlaid in its center. Also on the altar are a bottle of holy water (Jolt), a flask, and a holy tome (8.01 text). A gilded keyboard (Mac variety) sits at its base along with aluminum foil flowers (a donation from the wedding). The basic shape of the altar resembles an empty spool for wire.

Behind the altar, we have the donation box where collection is being taken to cover the costs of Cathedral construction. The donation box is a VT-100 monitor which has had its insides removed. Its clear face allows one to see the donations being made.

On each of the long empty pedestals in the lobby, sit gilded artifacts and relics. On the SE pedestal are several gilded monitors (one with its innards exposed for all to appreciate). On the NE pedestal is a vintage TEK oscilloscope. On the SW pedestal is a PDP style 19" rack complete with a 9-track magnetic tape drive, punch-tape reader, and disk drives. The NW pedestal sports many artifacts including a Wang daisy wheel printer sporting dual disk drives, circuit boards, disk packets, and magnetic tape.

HOUR OF STAR TREK
0.4-HONOR THY PROFESSORS
0.5-THOU SHALT NOT DECREASE ENTROPY

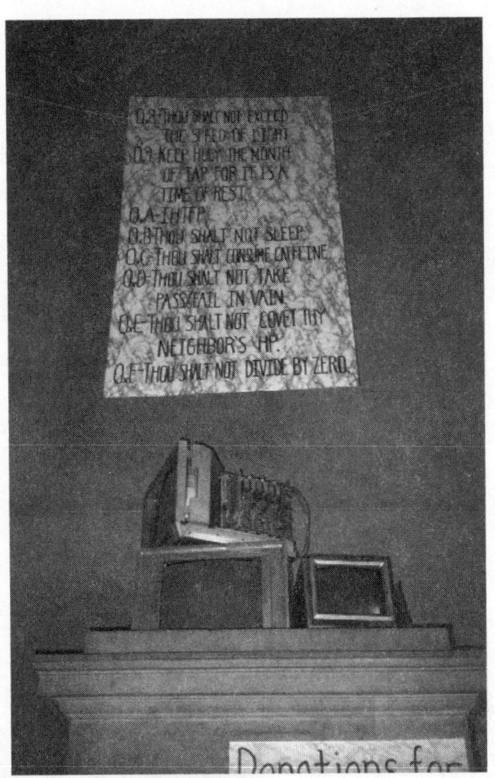
0.8-THOU SHALT NOT EXCEED
THE SPEED OF LIGHT
0.9-KEEP HOLY THE MONTH
OF IAP FOR IT IS A
TIME OF REST.
0.A-IHTFP
0.B-THOU SHALT NOT SLEEP
0.C-THOU SHALT CONSUME CAFFEINE
0.D-THOU SHALT NOT TAKE
PASS/FAIL IN VAIN
0.E-THOU SHALT NOT COVET THY
NEIGHBOR'S HP.
0.F-THOU SHALT NOT DIVIDE BY ZERO.

Donations for
building fund
much appreciated

The location of the coffee pot at the Donut Stand is labeled "Holy Water." The picture of William Barton Rogers has a light shining upon it and is labeled "Saint Rogers." Over the entrance to the Infinite Corridor is a sign that proclaims this place of Holy Tooling, "Our Lady of the All-Night Tool."

On the NE and SE walls are two stone tablets displaying the 0 × 10 commandments:

Tablet 1 [NE wall]

0×0 - I am Athena, thy Goddess. Thou shalt not have false gods before me.
0×1 - Thou shalt not take the name of OLC in vain.
0×2 - Thou shalt not eat at Lobdell.
0×3 - Thou shalt keep holy the hour of Star Trek.
0×4 - Honor thy professors, for they are the source of grades.
0×5 - Thou shalt not decrease entropy.
0×6 - Thou shalt not connect PWR to GND.
0×7 - Thou shalt not sex toads.

Tablet 2 [SE wall]

0×8 - Thou shalt not exceed the speed of light.
0×9 - Keep holy the month of IAP for it is a time of rest.
0×A - IHTFP.
0×B - Thou shalt not sleep.
0×C - Thou shalt consume caffeine.
0×D - Thou shalt not take pass/fail in vain.
0×E - Thou shalt not covet thy neighbor's HP.
0×F - Thou shalt not divide by zero.

Adorning each of the central pillars at the east end of the Cathedral are two paintings. One depicts an adoration scene in which an HP28S is the object of adoration; the picture is complete with 1700s clothing, cherubs, scrollwork, and inscriptions "Hackito Ergo Sum," "Liberty, Fraternity, Equality, Caffeine," and "Novus Ordo Seclorum." The other depicts a man torn between Athena (complete with helmet, spear, and owl) standing on a platform inscribed "The Temptation of Six" and another woman standing on a platform inscribed "The Path of Truth"—in the background are two terminals with wings flying about.

Father Eliza provides the Cathedral with an eternally vigilant spiritual overseer. He is available for Holy Confession all hours of the day or night. Father Eliza has had special training in the needs of the MIT community. Father Eliza's confessional resides on the south side of the Cathedral and allows private conversations between tools needing guidance and the Father (Father Eliza is running on an Apple II+). Unfortunately, the magnitude of some people's sins is sometimes too much for Father Eliza and he must be rebooted regularly. We believe he is getting stronger as the days pass and he becomes better acclimated to the MIT community.

CAFFEINE
HACKITO · ERGO · SUM

Under the Dome

The interior of the Institute's large dome is enclosed in the Barker Engineering Library and has lent itself to only a smattering of hacks over the years, but the small dome at Lobby 7, MIT's main entrance, has proven to be a high profile venue for many first class hacks. Among the most memorable:

The Starship Enterprise, 1989

When William Shatner visits MIT, hackers prepare a surprise. A replica of Captain James T. Kirk's starship hovers above Lobby 7 as if pausing before accelerating to warp speed.

Entertainment and Hacking, 1994

Hackers welcome incoming students with an alteration to the Institute's motto, which is carved in stone under the dome (see Making an Entrance).

Gargoyles, 1997

Hackers perch giant gargoyles under the dome (see Making an Entrance).

Paper Airplane, 1998

"Jolt is my copilot" is emblazoned on the side of this 30-pound "paper" airplane suspended above Lobby 7. Measuring almost 16 feet long and with a 7.5-foot wing span, this hack by "The Guild of Dislocated Hackers" coincides with the annual AIAA paper airplane contest. An entry-form for the craft is attached to a nearby pillar along with instructions for dismantling it.

Spider Web, Halloween, 1980s to present

Every so often a spider web will appear on campus—frequently, under the dome. Sometimes the web comes complete with spider bearing the name of an unpopular administrator.

Jolt Can, 1995

Jolt is described on the BBC website as the cola for "macho-nerds." With "all of the sugar and twice the caffeine," Jolt Cola has sustained many an MIT student through all-nighters. Just before final exams, hackers pay tribute to the drink of choice. The giant can "distributed by IHTFP Limited, Cambridge," bears authentic graphics and a list of ingredients: "Charles River Water, $Sugar^2$, Caffeine."

Paper Dolls, 2002

After a long period of renovation, the dome skylight is unveiled. Soon afterward, hackers accent the intricate glasswork with a ring of paper dolls.

Wheel of Tuition, 2002

On registration day for spring classes, the skylight is transformed into a wild game of chance with the spinner stopped at "Aid Denied."

"All Mondays Should Be So Beautiful": The Art of Hacking Art

What many in the MIT community think of as one of the great Lobby 7 hacks actually was not a hack at all—at least, it wasn't initially. The field of wheat that students and staff strolled through that Monday morning in May of 1996 actually was an art installation entitled "The Garden in the Machine." The wheat—nearly 100,000 stalks of it—was planted by artist Scott Raphael Schiamberg ('93, MA '96), a graduate student striving to invoke the grand American pastoral tradition with an intimate, small-scale oasis.

Because of its sheer ingenuity, surreal impact, and obvious impermanence, the MIT community assumed the wheat field to be a colossal hack. Not surprisingly, the project proved irresistible to real hackers, who soon contributed a cow and a scarecrow to the pastoral scene. Schiamberg's "hack" was covered by the media, from the newswires to the networks, but the artist most valued the visitor feedback. Fanmail flooded in via e-mail: "It took my breath away," one employee wrote. "All Mondays should be so beautiful."

The hackers' embellishment of the wheatfield was a tribute rather than a criticism, but hacks traditionally have served as a lively form of art criticism on campus. A common student lament is that MIT's taste in art is "big, black, and ugly." One of the students' least favorite pieces of sculpture is "Transparent Horizons" by Louise Nevelson. Students have objected that the enormous black steel structure intrudes on the East Campus dormitory courtyard and that dorm residents were never consulted about the choice or position of the art.

Not surprisingly, from its installation in 1975, "Transparent Horizons" has been the butt of numerous jokes. Over the years the two-story sculpture has been painted cheerful colors, covered in balloons, buried in snow, and once turned into a study carrel with a desk and floor lamp set atop one of its highest planes. In a 1981 hack, the work was rededicated with a new plaque:

Louise Nevelson / b 1900
Big Black Scrap Heap
1975

Elsewhere on campus sit two Alexander Calder sculptures "Big Sail" and "Little Sail." Hackers have adorned these two examples of "big black art" with smiley faces and once, in 1996, added an authentic-looking plaque dedicating a fictitious companion piece, "The Great Wind."

This last prank was the work of one of the most enduring MIT hacking groups, James E. Tetazoo (see Hacking Ethics). Tetazoo has demonstrated a penchant for art hacks over the years and has added artifacts to museum exhibitions from time to time—enhancements that have sometimes gone unnoticed by curators.

In 1979, Tetazoo installed a dime-store plastic aircraft carrier in a Hart Nautical Galleries exhibition along with a typical exhibit label with spoofed

text, a Tetazoo trademark (see U.S.S. Tetazoo). In 1985, at MIT's List Visual Arts Center, Tetazoo added its own installation to a contemporary art exhibition. Entitled "No Knife," the overturned wastebasket with cafeteria tray and incomplete place setting was not recognized as a hack by gallery workers for several hours. The "No Knife" exhibit was accompanied by a gallery label that attributed to the piece such artistically significant qualities as "temporary occasionalism," "casual formalism," and "sterile lateralism" (see No Knife).

But of all the art controversies in MIT history, the most heated has been the Great Hairball Controversy of 1990. In conjunction with MIT's 1% for the Arts program, a $75,000 art budget was allocated for the renovated Student Center in the late 1980s, and MIT commissioned Mags Harries to produce a sculpture for it. With the dual goals of involving students and evoking the essence of the Institute, Harries settled on a shaman's hat fashioned from the hair of MIT students. She divulged her underlying philosophy in the student newspaper *The Tech*: "Shamans were...the first scientists...the hats they wore, with four corners, which would be tied up together, were like a court jester's—the wise man and the fool speaking truths."

Promptly nicknamed "The Hairball," the sculpture quickly snowballed into a campus cause célèbre. The artwork was bound to be big and black and, many students felt, ugly too. According to the official plan, the sculpture would hang in the atrium between the first and third floors of the Student Center. Students lamented that the "hairball" would defeat the purpose of the renovations—to brighten the building and create an open atmosphere. Others were disturbed by the placement of the hair sculpture outside Lobdell, a student cafeteria. Inevitably the scheme inspired a spate of hacks.

When a steel frame prototype of the structure labeled "Sculpture Testing" was suspended in the Student Center atrium, hackers remarked on its resemblance to a cage by placing a plate of birdseed under the structure along with the sign, "Acme Roadrunner Trap." When the official testing sculpture was removed, they suspended an eight-foot-long functioning slide rule in the same space along with the sign, "Alternate Sculpture Testing."

Just before an open forum to discuss the artwork, students organized a reading of the Seussian spoof *Green Eggs and Hair,* which is reprinted in this book. Parodies of "official hairball propaganda" were disseminated around the campus. Following the style of the administration's memos on the subject, hackers created their own "Big Questions" (see Why Ruin the Atrium?). The protesters triumphed in the end—the hairball project never made it off the ground.

N

U.S.S. Tetazoo

Constructed in 423 B.C. by the Phoenician Turtle King Shii-Dawg, the Tetazoo's keel was laid four years later in Damascus.

During the Middle Ages she was put into drydock in Norfolk, Virginia, until 1490 when she returned to Spain to show Christopher Columbo the route to the Americas under the new name "Ninny," later misspelled by Spanish hysterians. Running low on rum, she detoured to Puerto Rico where the wreck of the Santa Maria can be seen to this day.

In the early 1800s, she became a privateer under Sir Harry Flashman, C.A.P., C.I.A., C.O.D. Lost to the Swiss Navy in fierce combat in the Inside Straits, she remained in their possession until 1905 when she was given to the U.S. Navy as spoils from the Russo-Japanese war.

During WWII, she served with distinction in the Atlantic, sinking seven submarines, many of them enemy. Captained by James Tetazoo, Sr., she was named in his honor after he died while making a still from an old depth charge. To this day, she serves with pride as the only (official) floating still in the U.S. Navy.

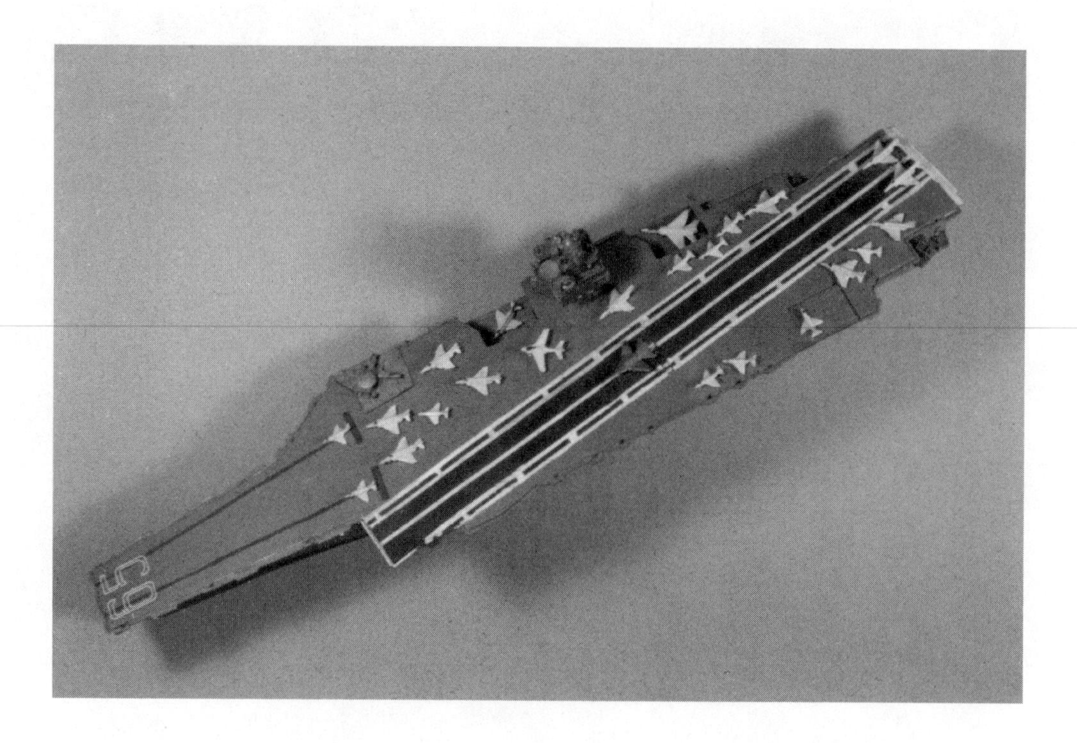

NO KNIFE
A STUDY IN MIXED MEDIA EARTH TONES, NUMBER THREE.

Realized by James Tetazoo December 1984

The artist's *mode d'emploi* relies upon minimalist kinematic methods; space and time are frozen in a staid reality of restrained sexuality. Temporary occasionalism, soon overcome throughout by symbolic nihility, pervades our earliest perception of the work. An overturned throwaway obelisk functions as symbolic pedestal; the work rests upon a manifestation of grey toned absence. Epicurean imagery is employed most effectively by Tetazoo; the glass, the porcelain, the plastic move in conflicting directions and yet are joined in a mood of stark pacifism. The sterile lateralism of the grouped utensils (*sans* knife), conveys a sense of eternal ennui, framed within the subtle ambience of discrete putrefaction. The casual formalism of the place setting draws upon our common internal instincts of existential persistence to unify us with the greater consciousness of human bondage.

Another
BIG QUESTION
about the Student Center Sculpture Project

Why ruin the atrium?

The Student Center Renovation Project was expensive—millions of dollars were spent transforming a dark, gloomy pit into a bright, trendy shopping mall.

Why spend $75,000 of the renovation fund to ruin the big wide-open "soul" of the building?

If Mags Harries really wants to find the proper place for this sculpture, maybe she should ask her friends over at the List Visual Arts Center if she can hang it in THEIR atrium. Students probably wouldn't mind the loss.

If Julius Stratton were alive today—and he is—he probably wouldn't like to know that the quotation plaque of his in the atrium will be partially obscured by the sculpture, and high above his bust a large hairball will hang.

Of course, it wouldn't be fair not to mention the conspiracy theory. That is, it could be that the ARA is secretly supporting the hair sculpture so that students will have something else to blame for hair in the food at Lobdell…

You will eventually stop complaining…

Green Eggs and Hair

Prior to an open forum to discuss the "Great Hairball Controversy," students organized a reading of a Seussian spoof, "Green Eggs and Hair."

I am art.
I'm made of hair.

That piece of art
That ball of hair
I do not like
That ball of hair.

Would you like me in Lobdell?

I would not like you
in Lobdell.
I do not want you
if you smell.
I do not want you
so you see,
I do not want you
over me.

Would you like me where you eat?

I would not like you
where I eat.
I do not want you
on my meat.
I do not want a ball of hair.
I do not want you anywhere.

Would you like me as a hat?

I do not want a
shaman's hat.
No superstition—
Nothing like that.
I do not want you so you see.
I do not want you at MIT.

Would you like me in your atrium?

In our atrium?
How could you dare?
You'll block the light
With your hair.

Fine. Fine.
Your point is clear.
You do not like me.
So I hear.

But I am art,
And I will be.
You will like me—
You will see!
(pause)

Would you like me
as a slide rule?
Thin and clear,
the engineer's tool?

Say!
I like a slide rule,
Thin and clear.
An object used
By the early engineer.
You're not superstitious,
You're not made of hairs.
And I do so like you
Over the stairs.

I do so like you,
And now I see,
That I would not mind you
At MIT!

Form + Function = Hack: The Architecture Hacks

MIT students have found hacking to be a medium equally effective for poking fun at campus architecture as it is for art. In 1988, for example, when the plans for the Stratton Student Center renovation were posted, hackers overlaid the rendering with a print of an M. C. Escher staircase that bore an uncanny resemblance to the actual design. In the same year, with a few cans of red, yellow, and green paint, they turned a vertical row of round windows in the new Health Services building into a giant stoplight.

The campus building that hackers seem to find most inspiring is alumnus I. M. Pei's 1985 futuristic box, the Wiesner Building, which houses the List Visual Arts Gallery and the Media Lab. As a harbinger of things to come, the dedication ceremony was met with a downpour of confetti that hackers had fed into ventilation ducts. Five pounds of shredded paper, 180 two-inch

strips of magnetic computer tape, and 175 fish-shaped paper airplanes spewed out over the atrium—and over MIT President Paul Gray ('54), who happened to be standing directly under the ducts when the barrage was launched.

Before the building even was dedicated, the ever-whimsical James E. Tetazoo added a mint green tile to the arrangement of oversized black, red, and yellow tiles adorning the building's façade, the work of artist Kenneth Noland. The extra square went unnoticed until the artist visited campus to view his work. The square was promptly removed. A few years later, hackers "rearranged" the order of the squares by placing colored panels over them, confusing the physical plant crew when they arrived to remedy the matter. At one point, the façade bore two red squares and one black. Eventually the art was put right, but the hacking continued.

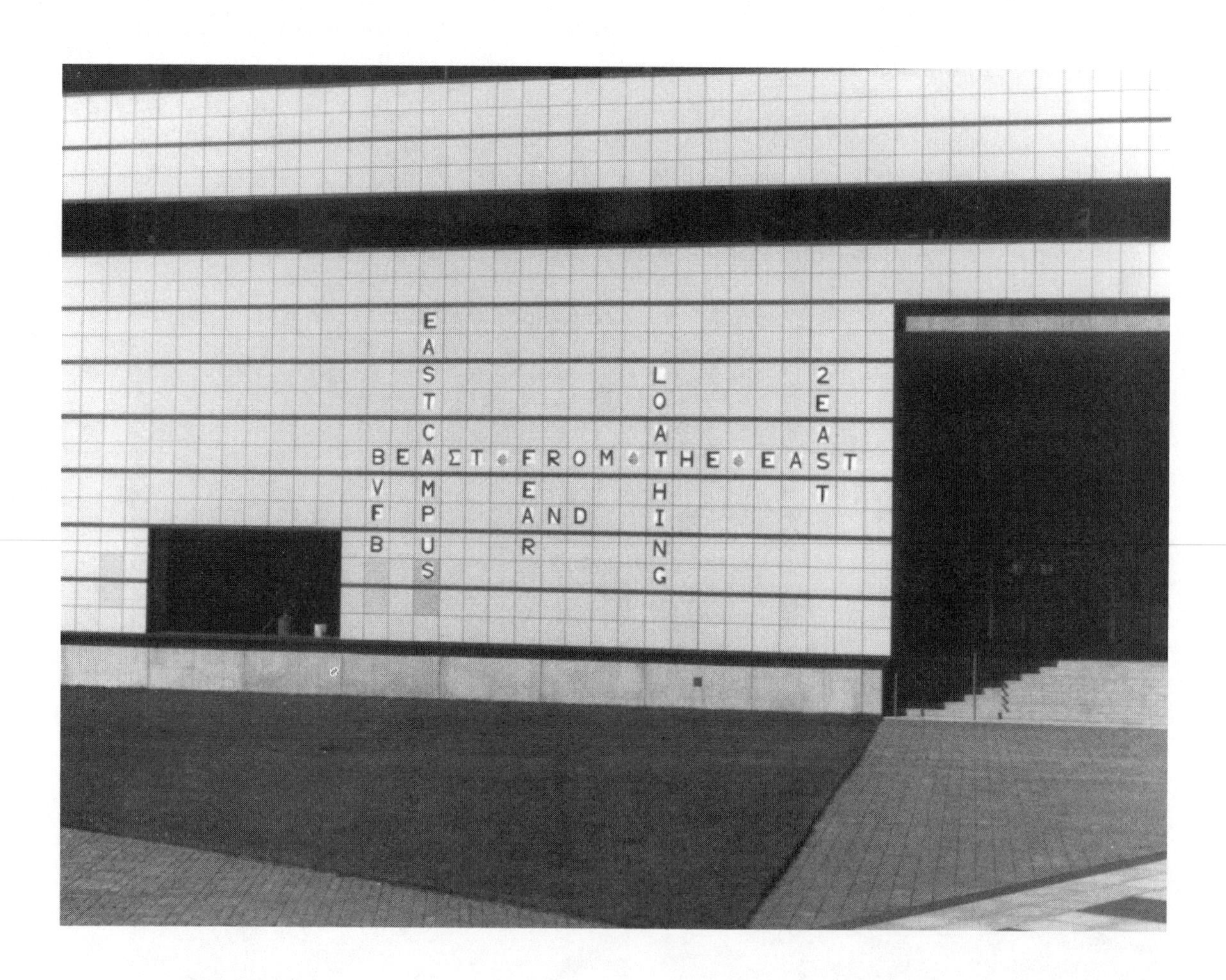

The next year, Jack Florey suspended a tire swing from the multistoried concrete arch that adjoins the building. On this same squared arch, hackers in 1989 installed a wide horizontal banner that read "Push Core for New Roll." This hack alluded to the fact that students, inspired by its white tile exterior, had dubbed Pei's architectural landmark "The Inside-Out Bathroom Building" and the "Pei Toilet," launching a multi-year spree of lavatorial hacks.

In 1994, hackers created a bathroom stall, using the installation as an opportunity to parody other campus issues. The door and walls were covered with MIT-related graffiti and a magnetic card reader was installed for acceptance of the "MIT Card," a debit card for students. Those using the "Pei Toilet" were instructed to run their cards through the slot to pay to enter and to exit the stall. An accompanying flyer described the toilet as a new Institute fundraising initiative.

Hackers took the lavatory theme a step farther with the 1995 "Scrubbing Bubbles" hack. Adopting the mascot of a popular bathroom tile cleaner, they installed the critters (enlarged to approximate scale) so that they appeared to be engaged in serious cleaning action on the white tiled exterior—a spruce-up, no doubt, for the building's upcoming tenth anniversary bash.

Perhaps it's I. M. Pei's spare aesthetic or that he's an alumnus, but hackers have had a particular inclination to embellish his buildings. The architect's design for Building 66, the Ralph Landau building, has inspired a succession of whimsical hacks since it was built in 1975. Generations of MIT students have gazed upon it, with its giant triangular footprint, only to see one thing: an ocean liner. The smokestack-like exhausts upon its roof only reinforce the illusion. During the building's dedication, residents of the neighboring East Campus dormitory showed their appreciation for the resemblance by lowering an anchor over the building's "bow," unfurling a banner christening the building the "U.S.S. Landau," and blasting "Anchors Aweigh" on their sound systems.

Pei's "ocean liner" has been adorned with several anchors in its history. In 1992, spectators were particularly impressed with a gargantuan anchor dangling from a thirty foot chain off the building's starboard side. Closer inspection revealed the four-foot-long links were actually fashioned from black garbage bags over wire. In 1998, in a nod to the first campus showing of the movie *Titanic,* hackers christened the building "The Techtanic" and suspended a giant beaver over the helm.

A Guide for New Employees: Building History and Numbering System

Buildings 66, E19, N2—yes, true to type, MIT identifies its buildings by cryptic numbers. Many of the buildings have names too, but most members of the campus community couldn't tell you what they are. This excerpt from the employee handbook takes a stab at explaining the arcane system.

If you have been trying to figure out the building numbering system here on campus, stop right here! Although not the best-reasoned system in the world, there is a certain, albeit limited, logic to the numbering of the buildings.

When MIT was built in 1916, the central group of buildings on campus was oriented toward the Charles River. The Dome Building, which is Building 10, with large foyer (Lobby 10), was meant to be the main entrance. All other buildings were arranged around Building 10, with the odd numbered buildings to the right as you face the river, and the even numbered on the left.

With this orientation, then, Buildings 1 and 2 were at the "front" of the campus.... Buildings 5 and 3, and 4 and 6 were arranged symmetrically behind them, with 7 and 8 in back of those, all following the odd-even arrangement around the central building, Building 10.

In 1938, the main entrance was moved to its present location in Building 7, located on Massachusetts Avenue. The Infinite Corridor, which extends all the way to the corner of Ames and Main begins here.

Infinite Corridor: MIT was designed so that people could move easily from building to building without going outside. The result of this planning was the Infinite Corridor, a 775-foot-long hallway that extends from the main MIT entrance in Building 7, through Buildings 3, 10, and 4, all the way to Building 8 and beyond.

And then there are the underground tunnels that parallel the infinite corridor but cross over Ames Street to buildings E19, E25, etc. These tunnels are high-traffic areas, especially in stormy weather. If you dare to venture down, just ask a colleague for the nearest entrance!

Although no longer the main entrance, Lobby 10 during the academic year hosts a daily bazaar of student and community activities—food; ticket sales; pottery, jewelry and crafts sales; blood drives; etc. The elevators for the central set of buildings are located just behind Lobby 10.

Lobby 7, the main entrance, has a culture of its own. It is the home of a student-run coffee and doughnut stand, which is open from 7 a.m. to 1 p.m.; a pick-up point for campus publications, such as *Tech Talk,* published every Wednesday by the MIT News Office, and *The Tech,* a twice-weekly student newspaper; and a constant display of banners advertising student activities from the balconies above. The MIT Concert Band's annual Halloween Concert takes place there. There is also an Information Center in Lobby 7 where you can get directions and maps and consult the large, detailed map posted on the wall.

West, East, and North Parts of the Campus

Buildings beyond the central area of the campus have numbers that are preceded by letters corresponding to compass points:

•W—to the west, across Mass. Ave. from the central buildings;

•N—to the north, across the railroad tracks that cross Mass. Ave. and parallel Vassar Street;

•E—to the east, across Ames Street, where the Wiesner Building and the medical center are;

•NW—to the northwest, across Mass. Ave. and beyond the tracks.

Thus, Building W20, the Stratton Student Center, is west of (across) Mass. Ave.; N51, the MIT Museum, is north of the railroad tracks; and the Wiesner Building (E15) and the Personnel Office (E19) are east of Ames Street. There is no system that explains the numbering of these buildings, so be sure to consult a map before you try to find one.

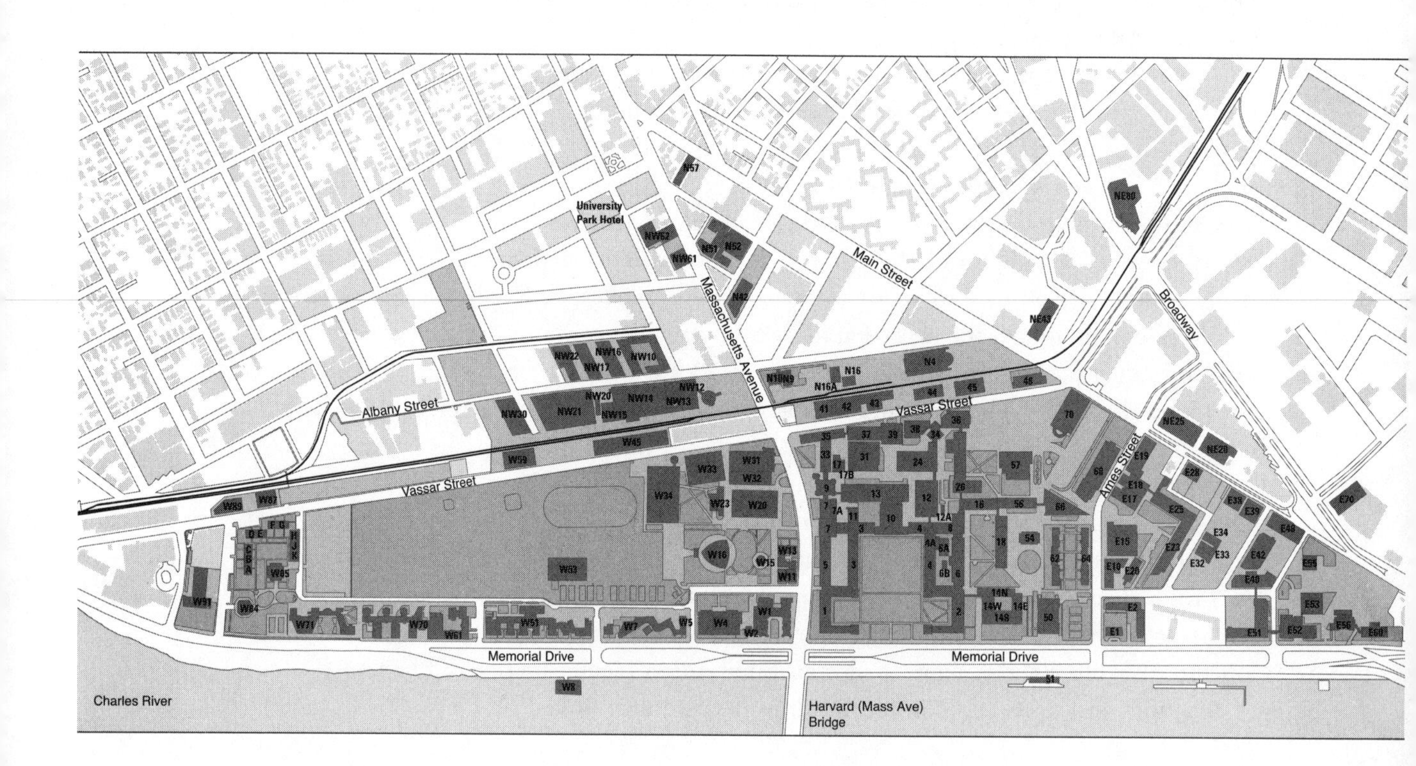

Hacking as Campus Commentary: The Editorial Hacks

MIT students view hacking as a handy editorial forum on the whole gamut of administration policies and procedures. One perpetual beef is housing. Like students at many universities, MIT students over the years have considered the living accommodations to be too scarce, too small, too expensive, and generally below par.

In 1970, residents moving into the newly unveiled MacGregor dormitory were beset with plumbing and electrical problems in the unfinished building. Paying tribute to the building's contractor, hackers added a realistic cornerstone to the new façade. It was inscribed "Jackson Sux." In 1994, when the renovation of the Building 14 wheelchair entrance was repeatedly delayed because of administrative snafus, hackers adorned it with a package that read, "Do Not Open 'Til Christmas 2014."

Responding to an ever-tightening housing crunch that same year, hackers launched an elaborate prank. After freshmen registered their housing preferences, they received what appeared to be an official letter. There were several variations, but each meandered in diplomatic jargon to the eventual bad news, which was presented with keen bureaucratic spin. An excerpt:

Dear Freshperson:

You will be happy to know that this year we have given more careful thought to the needs and desires of the students most affected by these arrangements. We have hired several specialists in undergraduate housing psychology and, at great expense to the Institute, we have devised some very exciting new options for several students. You are one of the lucky few randomly chosen to have their requests withdrawn from the normal housing lottery to allow you to participate in this innovative new housing experiment. We are confident you will find this to be a delightful educational experience and a pleasurable way to start your student career at MIT.

Specifically, we have arranged for you to room with five other persons in a four person police cruiser on top of the Great Dome. This living arrangement will provide you with a magnificent view of downtown Boston. Your accommodations will include free coffee *and doughnuts, provided daily by Campus Police via their traffic monitoring helicopters. Conveniently, this living arrangement provides quick access to 10–250, one of the most frequently used lecture halls for freshperson classes. You will also be glad to hear that, in winter months, you will be provided with gasoline to fuel the car for heating purposes. As an additional benefit, after the first month, you will be waived the $500 roof access fine....*

Sincerely,
Jack Florey, B.S.

Dean of Freshperson Housing Assignments

Institute housing administrators, with visions of freshmen heading up to the dome with all their worldly belongings, rushed to follow up with the official assignment letter, which began:

No, you haven't really been assigned to live in a police cruiser, a freight elevator, or the Chapel! If you received a message claiming this, or something similar, you've just encountered an MIT tradition known as a hack....

Two years later, hackers celebrated Halloween with another commentary on the housing situation. In an empty Plexiglas® display cube in the student center, they created a modular dorm room, complete with furniture, books, soft drink, Chinese food, and student dummy sporting a propeller beanie. A proposal posted on the outside of the 48-square-foot cube touted the "reengineering-inspired" Housing 2000 project as "a new housing paradigm to take MIT into the next century."

The escalating price of tuition has been a contentious issue, virtually since the day the Institute opened its doors, so it stands to reason that the annual "spontaneous tuition riot" is one of MIT's most enduring traditions. The "riot," which takes place on the day the rate hike is announced, consists of a motley collection of students wielding colorful signs along the lines of "$25,000 and Still One-Ply Toilet Paper!" or the simple "$25,000 is TDM" (too damn much), a perennial favorite.

On this hallowed day in 1993, when the Institute announced that a single semester's tuition was hitting the $10,000 mark, hackers "adjusted for inflation" the 13 × 30-foot one dollar bill mural on the MIT Cashier's Office. The hallmark of a good hack is painstaking detail and the $10,000 bill employed authentic markings from the 1918 series, including the likeness of Salmon P.

MIT HOUSING

Chase, father of the National Banking System (the government stopped printing $10,000 bills in 1946). Thanks to the application of a few basic engineering tricks, the original mural was not damaged in any way. While it appeared to replace the one-dollar bill, the new denomination was reproduced on stretched muslin mounted imperceptibly over the existing mural.

Hackers in 1998 used a less subtle approach to make their point about tuition inflation, greeting the incoming classes with a voluminous banner, "Welcome MIT Debtors."

Cafeteria fare is a student beef on most college campuses, and MIT is no exception. Aramark, the campus food service provider until recently, had been hacked from time to time, but 1995 was a particularly fruitful year. Inspiration came from two sources—the opening of the Biocafe in the new biology building and Aramark's penchant for gimmicky dining themes. On spring registration day, when MIT services traditionally set up information booths to answer questions and distribute materials, hackers set up a booth allegedly representing Aramark's most recent dining innovation—the Biohazard Café. Hackers in lab coats and chemical clean-up suits manned the booth, passing out menus, and encouraging booth visitors to sample "Soylent Green," "Lab Mice on Rice," and "Humungous Fungus Pizza"—provided they signed the release forms.

A more general disgruntlement is symbolized by the fire hose. Few students realize that MIT president Jerome Wiesner (1971–1980) actually—albeit inadvertently—launched this icon of disgruntlement when he said, "Getting an education from MIT is like taking a drink from a fire hose." Students instantly adopted the phrase and have reproduced it on banners and T-shirts ever since. During finals in 1991, hackers converted a fire hydrant into a fully functioning drinking fountain outside 26–100, the largest lecture hall on campus, so that students could literally "take a drink from the fire hose." The pranksters married a hydrant with a water fountain so that pressing the fountain's lever caused water to flow from a fire hose suspended over the fountain.

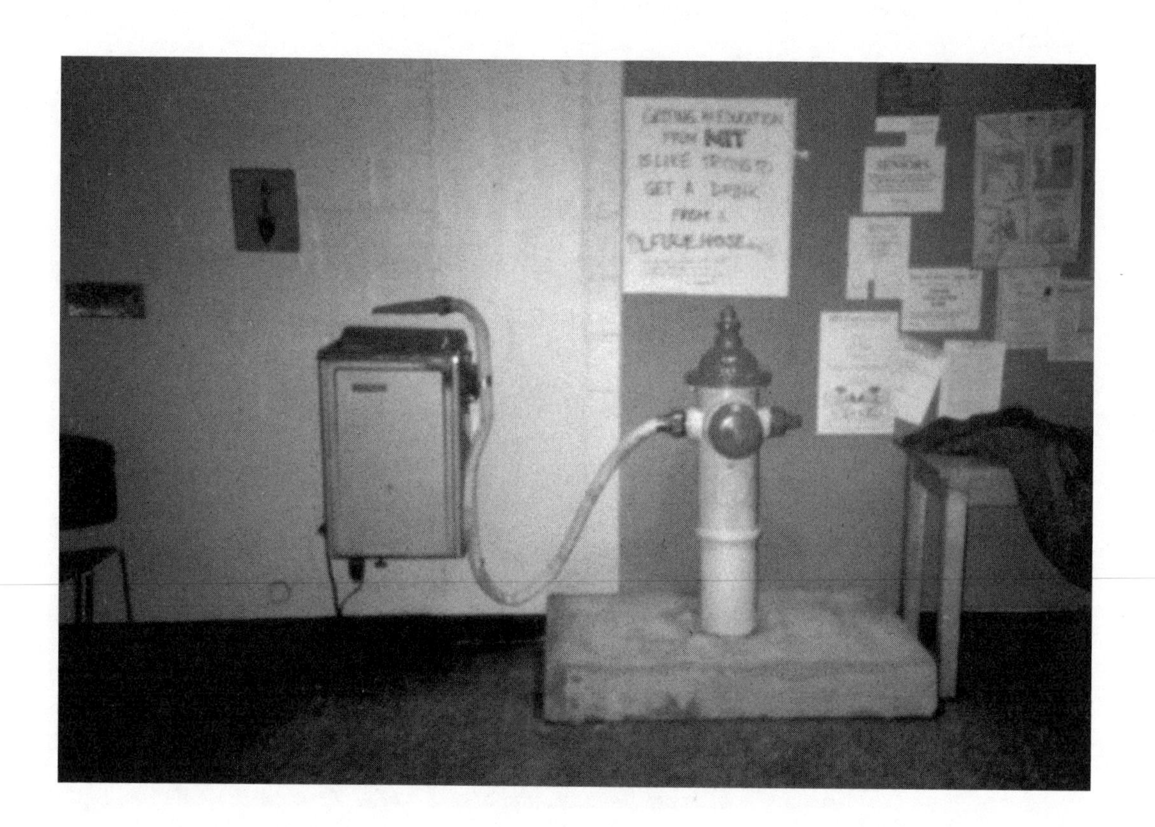

But the MIT administration hasn't been the only target of "editorial" hacks. Occasionally, hackers have been inspired to prepare a special welcome for auspicious Institute guests. When former vice president Al Gore gave the commencement address at graduation in 1996, he soon noticed that the assembled masses were diligently marking Bingo cards as he spoke. In fact, they were playing a game that hackers had distributed called "Al Gore Buzzword Bingo!" Instead of numbers, each square contained a familiar Gore buzzword. Whenever Gore uttered a word like "infobahn," "hybrid," or "paradigm," the students would check it off. "If you get five buzzwords in a row—horizontally, vertically, or diagonally—you have won Buzzword Bingo!" the instructions read. "Instead of shouting 'Bingo!' (which would be rude and potentially upset the men with wires in their ears...), hold up the card so that...the Vice President can see that you have won." Gore had been tipped off to the game, apparently, because when students cheered at one point in the speech, he quipped, "Did I say a buzzword?"

Microsoft has also seen its share of editorial hacks. In 1994, a hacking commentary on the software giant was as ubiquitous as Microsoft itself. Signs were posted throughout the main Institute thoroughfare using official Microsoft fonts, graphics, and logos with messages that made it seem the software empire controlled the world, from windows to doors, vending machines to toilet seats. Signs on stairways, for example, read "Microsoft UpwardConnect™ for Walkgroups vO.9Beta (not yet downward compatible)," and on vending machines: "Microsoft Dispens-O-Fud™ for YOU v32pi/3 (Think of our food as stock in our company, and invest your money here!)." When Gates visited two years later, hackers stretched enormous banners across some of the most prominent facades on campus. "MIT doesn't do Windows," read one. Another replicated the Windows95 signature "Start" button, substituting the word "Crash."

Al Gore Buzzword Bingo!

Welcome to Buzzword Bingo! For the past four years, most of you have enjoyed as a spectator the fine tradition of hacking at MIT. Today, as you finish your time here at MIT, you will have a chance to enjoy it as a participant. Soon, Vice President Gore will deliver an address on Distributed Intelligence. We will greet him with a Distributed Hack. Like any good distributed system, there will be no single point of failure, no single person whom the Campus Police or the Secret Service can stop.

As MIT students, and now as graduates, you are surely familiar with the tendency of non-technical people to use buzzwords when discussing technical issues. The Vice President, although more technically aware than most of his colleagues, is sure to use this technique in his speech. This hack is designed to gently remind him that he is at MIT, where we can see right through this strategy.

Below, you will find a Bingo board. This is similar to a regular bingo card, except that each square contains a buzzword instead of a number. When Al Gore uses a buzzword on your board, cross it off. If you get five buzzwords in a row - horizontally, vertically, or diagonally - you have won Buzzword Bingo! Instead of shouting "Bingo!" (which would be rude and potentially upset the men with wires in their ears and guns all over the place), hold up your card so that the other side faces the podium and the Vice President can see that you have won.

Have fun!

information superhighway	National Challenge	human-responsive	bitway	megaflop
Global Information Infrastructure	distributed	assimilation	vector	infobahn
empower	Information Age	FREE SQUARE	milestone	knowledge worker
NSF	communications	methodology	framework	environment
interoperability	virtual	environment	information space	mission goal

board id number = 1149160

MIT doesn't do Windows

Crash
ASSACHVSETTS·INST

A Sign of the Times: Hacking with Signs and Banners

The MIT community awaits hacks on April Fools' Day with the same anticipation that weather watchers look for Punxsutawney Phil on Groundhog Day. But when the campus population looked up expectantly at the Great Dome on April 1, 2000, they saw instead an enormous banner stretched across its august pedestal that read "Ceci n'est pas un hack." "This is Not a Hack," of course, being a wry play on Magritte's "The Treachery of Images."

Signs and banners are indeed one of the mainstays of hacking. In 1925, the practice began in earnest with an enormous electric Suffolk County Jail sign dramatically positioned on the face of the '93 dormitory, the scene of so many hacks perpetrated during this period. Throughout the century and into the next, hackers posted or transformed hundreds of signs. On one night in November 1987, for example, the large sign outside the Student Center advertising Starvin Marvin's Café at the Sala de Puerto Rico became "Salmonella de Puerto Rico Café," complete with a graphic of a squirming bacterium.

Spoofing MIT's tradition of numbering its buildings (see A Guide for New Employees), hackers in 1991 decided to erect their own sign for the upcoming dedication of the new Building E40. The authentic-looking plaque renamed the new addition to campus the "E. Phortey Building" in memory of "Edwin Phortey" and thanked "W. D. Phortey '40 and N. Dallas Phortey" for the funds necessary to make the building a reality.

In 1996, hackers replaced the regulation "No Trespassing" signs at the entrance to computer clusters with an edited version that appeared to be identical to the original—identical, that is, except for the addition of a graph and the message, "You must be at least this smart to use Athena workstations." The graph charted levels of intelligence in increasing increments starting at the low point, "Urchins who log in as root" and working up past "average Harvard student," "average B.U. student," and "average CalTech student," to the high point on the scale, "below average M.I.T. student."

During renovations in the Aero-Astro department in 2000, some employees had to be relocated to temporary facilities across from the building on Vassar Street. Hackers decided to boost the morale of those interned in the dismal mobile complex by posting a new sign on the chain link fence outside: "Aero-Astro Estates, A Trailer Community. It has been 71 days since our last tornado." The tornado count was updated regularly during the months the sign remained in place.

Details and authenticity are as essential in signs as they are in any hack. For that reason, the 1987 Nerd Crossing Sign is, in many ways, the gold standard of sign hacks. The bright yellow crossing sign, posted at the busy crosswalk at 77 Massachusetts Avenue, cleverly morphed a textbook nerd into the regulation graphics of a municipal crossing sign. Connoisseurs appreciated the

details: the regulation nerd backpack, a "nerd kit" (the kit used in electrical engineering labs), and a floppy disk—it was 1987, after all.

Then there are the banners welcoming freshman. Hackers usually give the incoming class a pithy orientation and the natural place to do this is at the annual freshman picnic. "Abandon All Hope Ye Who Enter Here," hackers warned in 1975, quoting the inscription on the gates of hell in Dante's "Inferno." In 1979, they quoted Poe: "For the Love of God, Montressor," the last words spoken by the character in "The Cask of Amontillado" as the final brick is put into place, sealing him into a wall forever.

In the entire panoply of sign hacks, one that still impresses as the decades pass, is the Sheraton Boston Hotel Sign. Back in the fall of 1967, members of the Alpha Tau Omega fraternity decided they needed to up the ante on marketing during R/O (residence/orientation week). That's the period when dorms, frat houses, and other living groups vie for first-years. A cadre of ATO frat brothers found their way to the mechanisms controlling the Sheraton Boston sign, a prominent landmark on the urban skyline positioned directly across the river from MIT. With the flip of a few switches and the aid of large black oilcloth, the hackers darkened all the letters except three—ATO. Since then, the Sheraton Boston has obligingly blackened its letters for ATO one night every year during R/O.

But the power of most sign hacks is that they speak for themselves. The following pages illustrate the broad range of banners and signs—silly and serious—that hackers have deployed over the years.

GO
SLOW
GEEKS CROSSI
AHEAD

M.I.T. monster
Eats
Boston / Back Bay

CHEW
MASSACHVSETTS
77
AVENVE

4-273
DEPARTMENT
OF
ALCHEMY

SLOW
GNURDS

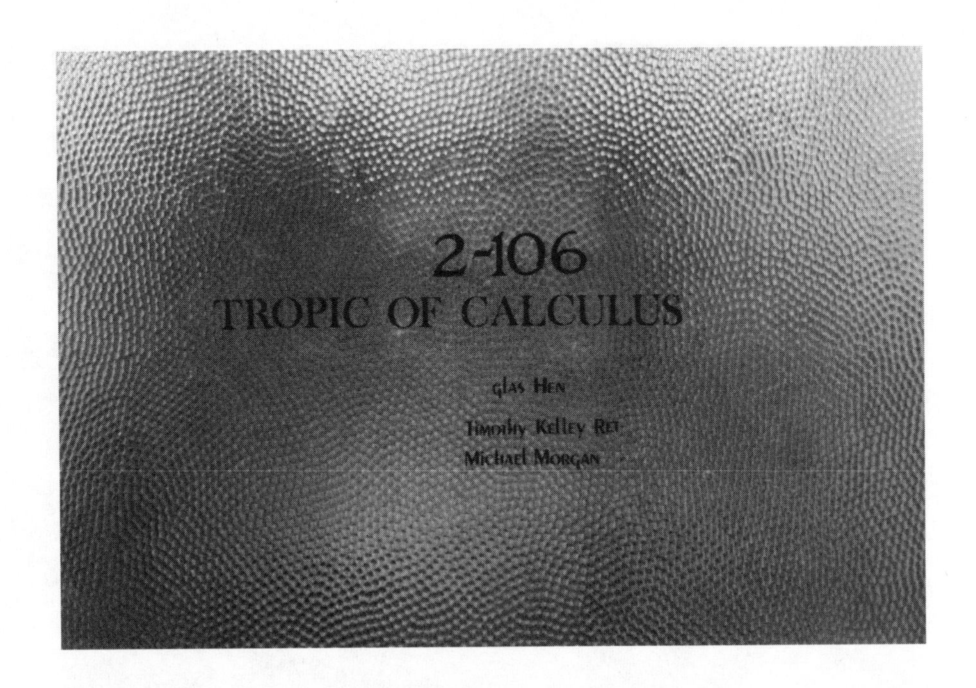
2-106
TROPIC OF CALCULUS
glas Hen
Timothy Kelley Ret
Michael Morgan

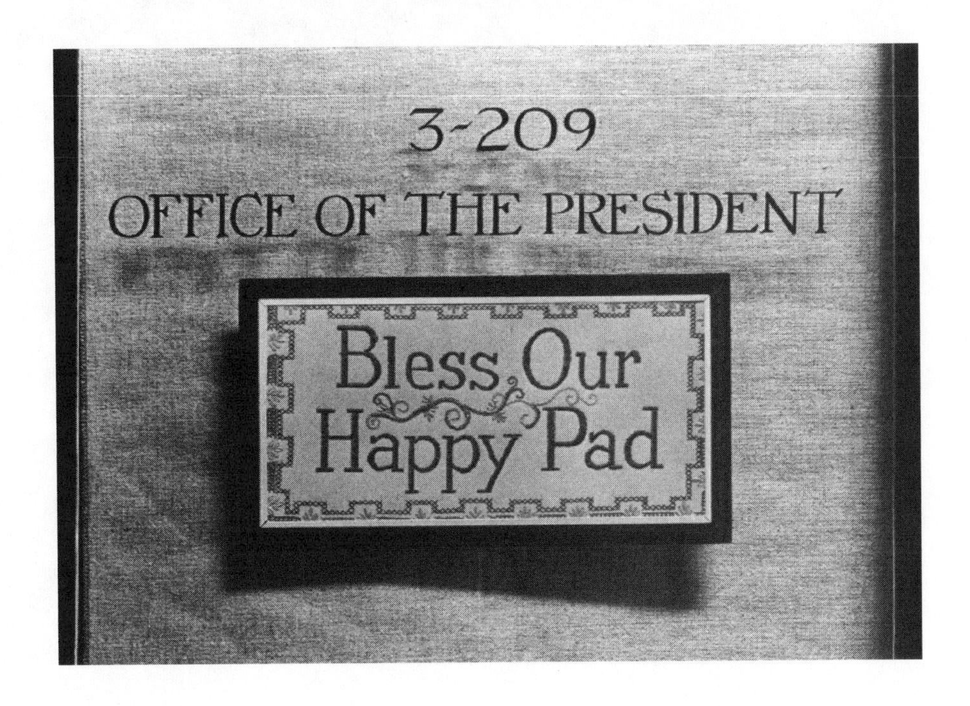
3-209
OFFICE OF THE PRESIDENT
Bless Our
Happy Pad

R/O CENTER
BAGGAGE SALE
STEREOS
17
CLOTHING

MIT

WELCOME TO HAHVAHD
MASSACHVSETTS INSTITVTE OF TECHNOLOGY

The Numbers Game: Hackers Reinvent Measurement

Numbers loom so large in the MIT culture, it's not surprising that hackers feel the need to work them from time to time. On April Fools' Day in 1972, for example, they published a handy manual called the "Alphabetic Number Tables" that spelled out and alphabetized all numbers 0–1000. "Availing ourselves of the unmatched technological facilities of this Institute," the introduction read, "we have developed, compiled, and revised these listings in the hope of bridging the cultural gap separating theoretical investigation and practical application." They hawked the manual for fifty cents in Lobby 10.

Apparently 1972 was a good year for numbers, because it also saw the birth of the Bruno measurement. The Bruno is the unit of volume equal to the size of the dent in the asphalt resulting from the six-story free fall of an upright piano. On October 24, 1972, the Bruno was 1158 cubic centimeters. Documented with microphones and high-speed movie cameras, the experiment revealed that the piano was traveling at 43 miles per hour, powered by 45,000 foot-pounds of energy at impact. The Bruno, by the way, was named for the student who suggested the experiment as a means for disposing of an old dorm piano. Although it has been repeated over the years whenever a campus piano passes its prime, hackers have disowned the practice as inelegant and destructive.

In 1997, hackers decided that the Institute's Infinite Corridor established a mathematical precedent. After all, the hallway—the longest straight corridor in the world—has been called "Infinite" for as long as anyone can remember. And since it is 47.2 rods long, it stands to mathematical reason that infinity must be 47.2 rods long. Thus it was expressed, deliberated, and converted to other units of measurement on posters and banners all along the Infinite Corridor (see Recalculating the Infinite Corridor).

The greatest measurement hack of all time is indisputably the Smoot—named for Oliver Smoot, the Lambda Chi Alpha fraternity pledge used to recalculate the length of the Harvard Bridge in 1958. It seems that Lambda Chi fraternity brother Tom O'Connor got it into his head to give his new pledges a chance to do public service. He figured that in making the long trek

ACME

← MIT
364.4 SMOOTS
PLUS 1 EAR

across the bridge from Boston, where the fraternity was located, some indicator of progress would be helpful when frat brothers held their heads down against the rain, sleet, snow, and hurricane force winds they regularly encountered en route.

Smoot, at 5' 7" was the shortest pledge among the freshman at hand and was thus elected to be the human yardstick. Using swimming-pool paint on the bridge sidewalk, the pledges notated every Smoot with a colorful tick mark, and every ten Smoots by spelling out the full measurement. Eventually, they reached the end of the bridge—at 364.4 Smoots plus one ear.

Every two years, Lambda Chi pledges repaint the markings, which Cambridge police officers have come to rely on for specifying exact locations when filling out accident reports. By some serendipitous twist, the progeny of both Smoot and O'Connor enrolled at MIT's Sloan School of Management 40 years later. Sherry Smoot found herself continually having to set the legend straight: No, for example, the lads had *not* been drinking.

Recalculating the Infinite Corridor

According to the signs posted along the Infinite Corridor during the 1997 "Implications of Infinity" hack, if the Infinite Corridor really is infinite, then...

The Harvard Bridge is approximately 120 rods across, so one must travel 2.5 times an infinite distance to walk across it. This might explain the attendance records of people from some of the ILGs across the river.

Length of Infinite Corridor:
655,633.4 Points

It takes the average student three minutes to walk from Lobby 7 to Lobby 8 down the Infinite Corridor. Since half of an infinite distance is the same length as an infinite distance, it would take two minutes to walk from Lobby 7 to Lobby 10, and another two minutes to walk half the remaining distance, and so on. It is therefore impossible to reach the eastern end of the corridor.

Length of Infinite Corridor:
447.918 Farad-Ohm-Knots

In order to reach Harvard starting from the center of the universe (Lobby 10), one must travel an infinite distance over 13 times! Since everything is within the universe, it is impossible to reach Harvard and therefore there can be no life there.

Length of Infinite Corridor:
214,935,769 BTU/Hectare atm

An MIT student can Rollerblade® down the Infinite Corridor, an infinite distance, in about a minute. This is faster than the Enterprise at Warp 10!

Length of Infinite Corridor:
96,675.13 Calories/Smoots^2 inHg

Beyond Recognition: Commemoration Hacks

While it is true that MIT hackers do not suffer fools gladly, they do have a sentimental streak. They rarely let an important occasion pass without observing it in some fashion—presenting William Shatner with scale model of the Starship Enterprise, for example (see Under the Dome). Some of the most memorable hacks over the years have commemorated holidays, celebrations, official visits, or just the start or end of school.

Hackers usually have something up their sleeves for incoming students. In fact, many of the hacks throughout this book have been created as a sort of initiation into the MIT culture. As President Paul Gray gave his annual speech welcoming incoming students in 1986, for example, Kresge Auditorium was suddenly filled with the strains of Bach's "Toccata and Fugue in D minor"—which would have been a pleasant diversion except for the unnerving fact that no one was seated at the pipe organ in the mezzanine.

In August of 1990, a photographer was organizing the class of 1994 on the colonnade just below the Great Dome for the class photo. After arranging and rearranging the crowd of students, he took aim. Suddenly, a vertical banner unfurled downward from the entablature high above. "Smile," it read, immediately followed by a deluge of 1,994 smiley-faced superballs. The balls bounced twenty or thirty feet into the air after the first impact just behind the assembled students; soon the air was alive with ricocheting spheres. None too pleased, the photographer shouted for attention, "Please stop throwing balls at the camera!" then ducked the resulting onslaught.

At the annual frosh picnic in 1994, hackers opted for a variation on the theme to initiate the Class of 1998. As the official Institute spokesman welcomed the incoming class, a twelve-foot balloon slowly inflated on the roof of Building 10 just below the Great Dome. Constructed of hexagonal and pentagonal plastic sheets taped together, and inflated with a leaf blower, the burgeoning balloon took the form of a fullerene molecule. To the assembled students, however, it looked like the world's largest soccer ball. The hexagons were painted with the letters "MIT," the pentagons with "IHTFP." The hack was probably also a nod to the World Cup Soccer championships that had been hosted locally over the summer.

SMILE

MASSACHVSETTS INSTITVTE OF TECHNOLOGY

ASSACHVSETTS INSTITVTE OF TECHNOLOGY

MASSACHVSETTS INSTITVTE OF TECHNOLOGY

SSACHVSETTS
STITVTE OF TECHNOLOGY

More than a decade before, in 1986, organizers of the frosh picnic schemed to sidestep the hacking distraction by moving the speeches to the more controlled environment of Kresge auditorium. Only first-years would be allowed. Alas, a strategically positioned hacker infiltrated the auditorium and directed more than fifty first-years to blow bubbles on cue during the President's speech. Soon the auditorium was filled with bubbles. As the luminaries seated on stage batted away the bubbles that were drifting their way, President Gray finished his prepared remarks.

MIT presidents have long been the target of hackers. When current president Charles Vest reported for duty on his first day on the job, he had the unsettling sensation of having misplaced his office. Vice president Constantine Simonides, who was escorting Vest, was even more dismayed, having a long knowledge of that particular hallway. Where they both believed the door should be, however, hung an enormous bulletin board covered with clippings hailing Vest's arrival. They soon realized that hackers had considered it their duty to commemorate the occasion (see The Case of the Disappearing President's Office).

Vest had come to the Institute from the University of Michigan in 1990, but his actual inauguration took place many months later, in May 1991. A hack would have been conspicuous by its absence at such an auspicious event, and hackers knew it. Inspired by Michigan's myriad satellite schools, they strung an enormous banner across the student center façade that read, in official UM font style and colors, "University of Michigan at Cambridge."

Whether turning columns into candy canes at Christmas or installing a shower stall in the computer cluster on April Fools' Day, hackers can usually be counted on to get into the spirit of holidays and celebrations—or invent them when necessary. During final exams in December 1994, hackers decided the time was never better to celebrate "Vector Day." The "Welcome to Athena" login banner on computer workstations at the Institute was replaced with the greeting "Happy Vector Day." Everywhere on campus, banners celebrated the holiday, and large vectors mounted on walls and over doorways pointed this way and that. In the vector calculus class, hackers distributed a commemorative assignment.

Commencement is a natural opportunity for commemorative hacks. Along with the 1996 "Al Gore Buzzword Bingo" prank, one of the most memorable graduation hacks in recent years was the 2001 "Parachuting Beaver" hack. Graduates sitting in Killian Court on that fine June day suddenly spotted a huge balloon drifting overhead. Shortly afterward, the sky was thick with parachuting beavers (the plush toy variety, of course). Carried off into the stratosphere by the balloon, the deployment mechanism washed up on Cape Cod a few days later.

Some of the most effective commemoration hacks have marked the passing of something or someone beloved. When MIT finally made preparations to tear down the barracks-like Building 20, which was built as a "temporary" facility during WWII, students recognized the demise of the fifty-year-old structure with an official-looking but surreally oversized "Deactivated Property" sign. The birthplace of many groundbreaking innovations during its fifty years, Building 20 was alleged to house a secret subbasement where great minds convened to change the world. After the building was torn down, hackers paid tribute to that legendary subterranean think tank by erecting an elevator on the leveled site, lending the impression that the hidden laboratories were still down there somewhere. In fact, a rumor persists on campus that the building is still standing but hidden by an invisibility shield.

When the Institute put an end to the thirty-three-year-old Rush tradition, hackers observed its passing with a variety of hacks. Rush, for the uninitiated, was the period during which freshman made a decision about where to live. During this time, they were courted royally by dorms, independent living groups, and fraternities. In conjunction with sweeping changes relative to student housing, however, the practice was discontinued in 2001.

That fall, hackers solemnly commemorated Rush. On the entablature under the Great Dome, they hung a wide, wistful banner, "So Long and Thanks for All the Frosh." The banner was positioned so as to be a prominent feature in the annual class photo, which was happening on the steps below. New students must have wondered what they'd missed with the passing of Rush, because as they mugged for the photographer, a funeral procession then emerged across Killian court. A trumpeter playing "Taps" headed the procession followed by a group of students dressed in black. They in turn were followed by pallbearers carrying a massive tombstone inscribed, "RIP RUSH 1968–2001." The mourners held a brief service, then moved on, leaving the tombstone behind for the new students to puzzle over.

RIP
RUSH

RIP
RUSH
1968-2001

The "Fishbowl" was a communal computer cluster of twenty-nine workstations, named for its large plate-glass windows that overlooked the Infinite Corridor. When the MIT administration decided to relocate the cluster as part of a consolidation of student services, hackers organized a formal lament. First, with a few pieces of jagged Plexiglas®, they gave the impression that a rock had been thrown through the Fishbowl and that water had spilled into the hallway. Paper fish appeared to flounder among the puddles. Wet footprints tracked to the Student Services Office (the department held responsible for the move) and a plate of paper sushi was left at the door. The coup de grâce was the login symbol on Athena, the campus computer network—hackers replaced the standard owl icon with an ailing fish, its tail twitching in the final spasms of death. It being the impact-aware 1990s, hackers followed up with both computer and physical plant staff on how to erase the hack, but officials took them up on their offer to put it right themselves. In a letter to hackers, the computer cluster supervisor noted that "Student Services has been reported to APCF, the Association for the Prevention of Cruelty to Fish."

Hackers were compelled to commemorate two somber events in 2001. A few days after the death of science fiction writer Douglas Adams, they strung a banner under the Great Dome thanking him for his wit. A few days after September 11, they posted a massive 25 × 16-foot American flag in the same spot.

Object Lessons: Hacks in the Classroom

From the time that students sprinkled explosives on the drill room floor in the 1870s, the MIT classroom has been a hotbed of pranks. One bright fall day in 1985, students filing into their physics lecture took what they thought were the usual handouts at the front of the room. When they sat down and reviewed the day's assignment, however, they found that a class hack was afoot. The handout, parodying typical class assignments, supplied detailed instructions for the construction and launch of a paper airplane. The hack went off without a hitch and at precisely 11:15, the lecturer ducked as hundreds of paper airplanes shot toward him. Perhaps hackers were celebrating the work of alumnus Charles Stark Draper, Class of 1926—the National Society of Professional Engineers had only a few months earlier cited his invention of inertial guidance as one of the ten outstanding engineering achievements of the previous fifty years.

Hackers employed the "mock assignment" method again in May 1992. Students showing up for their Structure and Interpretation of Computer Programs class ("6.001") gathered the handouts at the front of the hall then took a seat. When they glanced at the materials, they realized one of the course materials was actually a hack. Entitled the "6.001 Spellbook," it proceeded to detail a series of computer hexes that may have seemed all too real to many of the students in this challenging course.

During the 1992 presidential election, first-years in the multivariable calculus class of Hartley Rogers Jr. decided that he was their man and launched a campus-wide campaign to get him elected. Playing on Rogers' pet phrase, they adopted the campaign slogan, "Hartley Rogers: The *Intuitively Obvious* Choice for President." During the campaign, students covered the projection screen above the lectern with campaign posters that remained hidden until Rogers lowered the motorized screen at the end of class. On election day, hackers deployed a remote-controlled car fashioned to look like the trolley from "Mr. Rogers' Neighborhood." It sped around the lecture hall accompanied by the strains of the Hartley Rogers campaign song, the "Mr. Rogers" show theme.

MASSACHUSETTS INSTITUTE OF TECHNOLOGY
Physics Department

Physics 8.01 — October 25, 1985

ASSIGNMENT No. 7.1
(Do 11:15 a.m., Friday, October 25)

Reading Assignment for Week no. 7:
Review of airplane tossing technique, Chapter 22.5.
Advanced folding technique, Chapter 22.7.
Infra-red tracking and guidance techniques, Chapter 23.2.

Material Covered in Lecture this week:

Friday, October 25	Ready
Friday, October 25	Aim
Friday, October 25	Fire
Monday, October 28	First Aid

(special topic: treatment of paper cuts.)

Special Reminder:
The final exam in paper airplane construction and launch will be held (during the lecture time) on Friday, October 25. You will be held responsible for the material covered in chaplers 22-3 (i.e. this homework,

Problem 7.1-1: Paper airplane construction.
If you don't know how to make one by now, you're probably beyond hope, but as Airplane construction is only a minor subtopic, I have included a diagram of the necessary folds as well as the final product. You may use this paper. Extra credit will be given for creative designs.

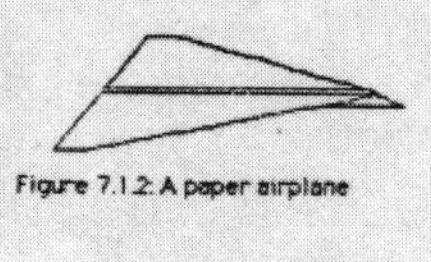

Figure 7.1.2: A paper airplane

Figure 7.1.1: Folding diagram

Problem 7.1-2: Paper Airplane Launching.
As its name suggests, this step involves the launching of the planes designed in problem 7.1-2. The goal is for the entire paper airplane fleet to impact the general vicinity of Professor Meyer at a given time. This involves proper launching technique to maximize the distance function with respect to force, and thus, the range of the airplane. Completing this problem will necessitate drawing a free-body diagram of the plane, including air resistance and lift, as well as a rapid measurement (to within 3 microns (1 micron = 1X10^{-6}m) accuracy) of the distance from your seat to the stage. As our goal is to minimize error, we must make many simultaneous trials of this experiment. Hint: throw it at the professor.

IMPORTANT NOTE: The launch is to take place at precisely 11:15 a.m. according to the room clock. Please have your equipment ready to by then. Fnord.

Though students knew their candidate would not receive a statistically significant number of votes, the musical tribute drew a standing ovation from the class. By odd coincidence, many years earlier, Rogers was nominated for fifth-grade class secretary by none other than Barbara Pierce, who went on to marry a man named George Bush.

Why Sleep through a Class When You Can Hack It?

Snappy Assembly, circa 1870

Pranksters sprinkle iodide of nitrogen, a mild contact explosive, on the drill room floor lending snap, crackle, and pop to routine assembly.

Progression of Tardies, 1927

Although vowing that he would never shut the door in a man's face, a professor religiously locks the classroom at five minutes past the hour to discourage late arrivals. One day, students wait until five minutes after the bell, then trickle into the room at carefully spaced intervals so the professor can never close the door—at least not for another twenty-five minutes.

Casual Saturday, 1949

Students arrive at their early Saturday morning class in robes and pajamas to protest the cruel and unusual scheduling.

Exam a la Carte, 1978

A student throws a red checkered tablecloth over his exam table, sets out bottles of wine, corkscrew, glass, a plate of bread and cheese, and regulation No. 2 pencils, then settles in and takes the test.

Reversal, 1982

Industrious hackers reverse all 199 seats in the 2–190 lecture hall so that they face the back of the room. The prank is all the more ambitious because the seats are bolted to the floor.

Paper Airplane Assignment, 1985

Students pick up the usual stack of handouts as they enter the lecture hall, only to find that one is a hack. The sheet gives detailed instructions on how to make a paper airplane…and when to launch it at the lecturer.

Turbojet, 1987

Hackers move the massive turbojet on display in another building to the front of the unified engineering class. On the lecture hall blackboard, they ask, "Can You Say Turbojet?"

Giant Clack Balls, 1988

One morning, students and faculty arrive in one of the principal campus lecture halls to find an enormous collision ball apparatus suspended at the front of the classroom.

Chalkboard Gremlins, 1981 and 1992

Using a handmade radio-controlled device, a hacker raises and lowers the lecture hall chalkboards to the frustration of the lecturer in the 10–250 lecture hall.

Hartley Rogers for President, 1992

Students draft their multivariable calculus teacher for President of the United States (see Object Lessons).

6.001 Spellbook, 1992

A spoof on fantasy role-playing incantations, hackers distribute a "spellbook" to students that explains why some of their computer programming experiments may be going awry.

Worth a Thousand Words: Hacks Fit to Print

Of course, MIT is not *just* about numbers. The Institute is proud of a powerful, if quirky, literary legacy that includes award-winning novelists, poets, playwrights, science fiction writers, and even authors of children's literature. Civil engineering alumnus Hugh Lofting, a student at the turn of the century, wrote the Dr. Dolittle books. So literary hackers—and not a hack among them—have had plenty of inspiration.

Literary hacking, in fact, can be traced all the way back to 1939, when an alumnus from the class of 1889 penned the novelty novel "Gadsby," a 50,110-word saga that did not contain a single "e." In fact, the author tied the "e" key down on his typewriter to avoid any inadvertent slips.

According to *Gadsby*, "Youth cannot stay for long in a condition of inactivity," and thus it is with literary hackers. Throughout MIT's history, hackers have been prolific authors, publishing, among other works, parody magazines, posters, and brochures. The one thing they all have in common is obsessive attention to detail—each spoof copies the graphics and materials of its subject to the letter. Often, these hack pieces are mistaken for the original before the reader realizes, for example, that the official currency of the "Peoples Republic of Cambridge" is probably not changing to the ruble.

Especially during the 1990s, hack publications were nearly as ubiquitous as the ones they parodied. The student newspaper *The Tech* was spoofed on many occasions including *The Absolut Tech, The TeX Files, The Wreck,* and *The Dreck.* The Institute's primary newspaper *Tech Talk* has been lampooned many times over the years, often with the sporadically annual spoof *Tich Tolk.*

A variation on the print hack theme is the print hoax, a good example of which is Professor Catesbiana's regular letters to the editor in the 1970s. This prolific, opinionated, but entirely fictional MIT professor made a point of taking a bizarrely contrary position on random issues of the day. In a letter to the *Boston Globe*, for example, he complained when windows replaced sheets of plywood on I. M. Pei's famous John Hancock building. "It was distinct," Catesbiana lamented, "Now, alas, it is just another skyscraper." The invention of MIT hackers, Catesbiana (the scientific name of the American bullfrog) was assigned an office in the MIT lab where bullfrogs were kept for research on amphibian immune systems.

And then there's *VooDoo*, the sporadically published campus humor magazine that's been spoofing life on campus and off since 1919. The boundaries of *VooDoo* humor have always reached well beyond the pages of its magazines. *VooDoo* stunts over the years have included a variety of elaborate hoaxes and publicity stunts, including a wild spree with a gorilla in a helicopter (see That VooDoo That You Do).

That VooDoo That You Do

VooDoo, "MIT's only intentionally humorous campus publication since 1919," has drifted in and out of print over the years. Especially in the period just before and after World War II, however, it single-handedly raised the bar for campus pranks. Of course, the publicity stunts *VooDoo* pulled to sell magazines may not, by strictest definition, qualify as hacks, but they were born of the Institute hacking culture and they powerfully influenced it. A sampling:

Wellesley College Coup, 1947

Listeners enjoying a Beethoven piano sonata on the Wellesley College radio station are alarmed as the music abruptly halts and is replaced by the ominous sounds of a studio ruckus. Suddenly a male voice announces plans to set up "an electromorphic flux and contrapolar micro-reflector with which to create neutral mesons to blow up the college." His speech is followed by a commercial for *VooDoo* magazine. The incident doesn't cause quite as much of a stir as the event it spoofs—Orson Welles "War of the Worlds"— but the press soon arrives to photograph the MIT hackers and the good-natured Wellesley announcers they have tied to chairs.

Dipsy Duck, 1948

The magazine constructs a 12-foot-long "hydroelectric" Dipsy Duck, reporting it to be a prototype for the 250-foot-long Dipsy Ducks that will soon be installed beside rivers to generate electricity. The jig is up, however, when a motor is found to be powering the Dipsy prototype.

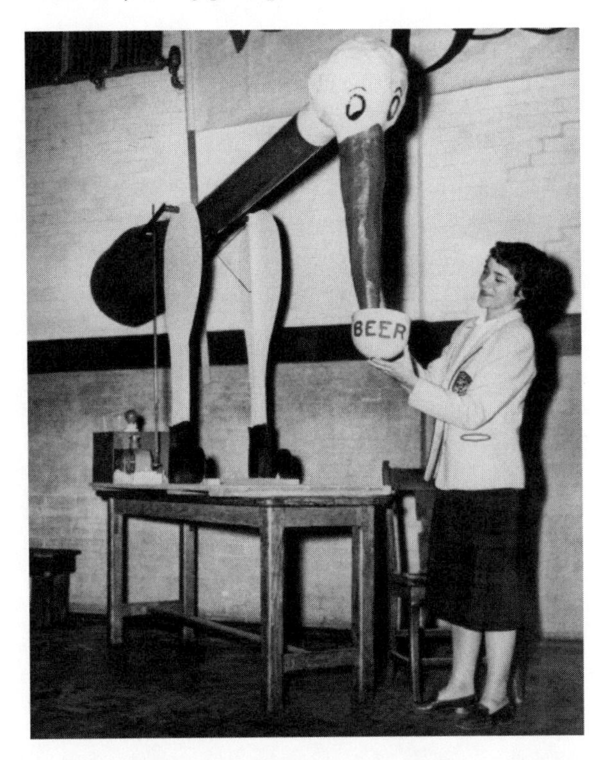

Pseudo Scientific American, 1958

To celebrate the inaugural issue of *Pseudo Scientific American* magazine, *VooDoo* constructs a time machine. On the test drive of the gadget, they decide to bring back the first Boston city planner. When the dust clears, a spotted calf appears—a play on the conventional wisdom that most of Boston's winding streets are paved cow paths.

VooDoo Goes Ape, 1965

Drawn by the anticipation of a good contest, crowds gather in Killian Court to see the first annual American Faunch Championship—sponsored by *VooDoo*. The magazine claims that the game dates back to the ancient Aztecs and is similar to soccer, with the primary exception of human goal posts. As police contain a burgeoning crowd, the game begins but soon comes to a halt as a helicopter descends on the playing field. It hovers over the ground briefly. Then a gorilla leaps out and tries to buy a copy of *VooDoo* from one of the players. When he learns the price has increased by a nickel to forty cents, a melee ensues. In the confusion, the gorilla grabs the issue, pummels several of the players, and then departs the same way he arrived. The helicopter disappears over the Great Dome and peace reigns once again on the playing field.

Teaching a Nation to Make Snow: Hoax Hacks

At a school where gorillas leap out of helicopters to pick up a copy of the campus humor magazine, it is not overstating the case to say that successful pranks are often elaborate affairs—no more so than the hoax hacks.

In January 1968, students from the Baker House dormitory reported a new engineering breakthrough to the press. By throwing open the windows and turning on the showers full force, they said they had found a new way to make snow. The *Boston Herald-Traveler*, one of the major Boston dailies, ran the story and photo on page one. From there, the wire services picked it up and before long, the story swept the nation. Unfortunately for the media and those who tried to duplicate the experiment in homes and dorms across America, the story was a hack.

As hacks go, this one was actually a bit of an accident. Students had brought snow into the showers to make a snowman. Finding it too dry, they turned on the showers to create steam to make the snow more pliable. When the steam began to overwhelm, they opened the windows. The resulting foggy, slushy, snow scene struck them as so phantasmagorical, it warranted a photo. And the photo was so exceptional, they felt it warranted a hack.

For their part, the hackers were surprised at the gullibility of the press. "Anybody knows that if you mix hot water and cold air," said one student, "the only thing you'll get is a cold shower."

A little more than twenty years later, in 1989 a small group of MIT hackers undertook a high-risk, high-profile hack without having to create a single prop. The aim was to shake the credibility of tabloid TV. At a student broadcasting conference, one of the hackers approached the executive producer of the Morton Downey Jr. show, posing as a Harvard student and member of the North American Man-Boy Love Association (NAMBLA). The producer, thinking the topic would be ideal for ratings sweep week, took the bait and asked for literature about the organization. The hacker then requested materials from the NAMBLA organization and forwarded them on.

On the night of the taping, the hacker was seated next to Dr. Joyce Brothers as a chain-smoking Downey pummeled him with questions and insults, at one point tearing the NAMBLA brochure to bits. The audience was equally hostile, with one man shouting, "What they did to Ted Bundy, I'd do the same thing to you!" After the syndicated show aired, the hacker revealed the ruse to the media. In an interview in a local newspaper, he said, "My next step is to get on Geraldo, but I'm probably blacklisted from trash TV."

If it weren't for the fact that a 1998 Web page hoax happened on April Fools' Day, hackers might well have tricked a few people into thinking that a Fortune 500 company had bought a world-class educational institution. In response to MIT's increasing relationships with Disney, hackers were inspired to break into the MIT web server and "Disnify" the home page. As a result, Mickey Mouse, in his Sorcerer's Apprentice costume, appeared to have conjured up a pair of mouse ears for the Great Dome. The banner headline "Disney to acquire MIT for 6.9 Billion" linked to a press release that announced "Top-Ranked Engineering School Will Switch to Imagineering"

The MIT administration quickly responded with its own press release, "'*Disney buys MIT* Hack Revealed by Low Price...." In the release, MIT spokesman Ken Campbell noted that the Mickey Mouse Club theme song had long been a tradition at MIT, with the letters "MIT...Ph.D... M, O, N, E, Y..." substituted for the spelling of Mickey's name.

"Please Wait to Be Served": The Performance Hacks

Sometimes a propeller beanie set jauntily atop the Great Dome says it all, but every now and then, a procession, a kidnapping, or even a boiling cauldron is called for. In the vernacular, these "happenings" are known as "performance hacks." From mock swordfights to chanting monks, performance hacks are an enduring Institute hacking tradition.

In 1978, two MIT traditions were melded to create one of the most beloved performance hacks of all time. Since 1953, the Institute had been crowning the Ugliest Man on Campus. The U.M.O.C. is actually a charity event held by MIT's service fraternity, Alpha Phi Omega. The "ugly man" who collects the most money for charity is declared ugliest of them all. In 1978, the winner was also named homecoming queen for MIT's first (in modern times) home football game. The spectacularly ugly U.M.O.C. (pronounced "you mock"), holding his cane aloft, rode into the stadium on a gargantuan float—a replica of MIT, complete with its own somewhat misshapen Great Dome. The 1978 U.M.O.C.'s bid to become national homecoming queen was thwarted when event organizers refused to allow him to enter the contest.

In 1996, the Order of Random Knights hacking group decided that Halloween was the ideal time for a performance hack. They made a goodwill tour of the campus, picking up the dead. Inspired by a scene in *Monty Python and the Holy Grail,* the hackers donned black robes and pushed wheeled carts piled with bodies around campus—the bodies, of course, belonged to fellow hackers.

Hackers sometimes pull off a performance hack to orient a new class of students to life at the Institute. Tradition has it that MIT upperclassmen take groups of first-years out for dinner on their first evening on campus to introduce them to the local eateries. They hold signs aloft with their intended destination—"Sushi Express," for example, or "TGI Fridays." During orientation in 1993, "Cannibals at MIT" offered frosh an alternative dining experience.

A "Cannibal" in a chef's hat stirred an enormous cauldron while a table nearby was set for dinner. "Please wait to be served," patrons were instructed.

Towering over the entire tableau was an enormous sign

Cannibals at MIT
We would like to have you for dinner!

Wearing club T-shirts, the Cannibals darted through the crowd measuring freshmen in search of the "perfect specimen." Those who passed muster were carried over and stuffed into the pot. When the pot was full, the Cannibals danced around it:

Frosh be nimble, frosh be quick,
Cook frosh up on a great big stick!

and

Double, double, toil and trouble
Fire burn and freshmen bubble!

In 1997, inspired by the movie *2001: A Space Odyssey,* hackers dressed as big, black, hairy apes and carried a massive black monolith into Killian Court during the freshman picnic. Apparently, their aim was to encourage the Class of 2001 to evolve into higher life forms during their years at MIT.

When the opportunity presents itself, hackers like to orient parents to the MIT culture, too. During Parents' Weekend in 1991, they chose an appropriate venue—Institute hack archivist Brian Leibowitz's official lecture for freshmen and their families. The lights went down as Leibowitz prepared to discuss the first slide.

Suddenly, ushered in by a loud, booming rumble, a contingent of commandos, dressed entirely in black, invaded the 10-250 lecture hall and grabbed an unsuspecting student. The commandos claimed to be representing SPODSA, "The Secret Police of the Office of the Dean for Student Affairs." This was a clear slam at the ODSA for what students considered to be policies aimed at giving them fewer freedoms. Two of the commandos read an arrest warrant detailing the first-year's nerdly crimes, which included caffeine abuse, accepting financial aid, and attending a lecture on hacking.

In a scene reminiscent of the abduction of Joe Buttle in the movie *Brazil,* the unsuspecting student was stuffed into a body bag and carried away. Leibowitz was then asked to sign a receipt for her return, sign for his copy of the receipt, and for the commando's copy of Leibowitz's copy of the receipt.

A few months later, Leibowitz attempted to give the talk again. As the event progressed, the pitch of his voice slowly crept skyward. About 15–20 minutes into the talk, his pitch was one half-tone above normal. As it turned out, hackers were controlling his operatic tenor with their own audio hookup, which they had patched into the lecture hall sound system, running the microphone input signal through a mixing board that included a set of pitch shifters.

Leibowitz could not hear the audio feed over the sound of his own voice, however, and had no idea his pitch was climbing higher and higher. Puzzled by the laughter that was preceding every punchline, he did not learn until the talk was over that the sound had been distorted. The sound technicians running the lecture series discovered the hack and fixed the problem, but hackers weren't ready to call it a night. Shortly afterward, an unidentified telephone began to ring on stage. The speaker frantically searched for the source of the din and finally located the phone hidden is a nearby podium. When he answered it, the hacker on the other end ordered a pizza for delivery to 10–1000 (the unofficial room number of the Great Dome). Leibowitz replied curtly that the location was outside of his delivery range and continued his talk without further interruption.

Occasionally, performance hacks are directed at an audience outside the community, as in 1976 when hackers besieged a bus full of tourists making the usual trip down Amherst Alley to view the "natives." Hackers, pretending to be fending off alien invaders, attacked the bus with suction cup arrows, *Star Trek* phasers, and other weapons. Students maintained that tour bus traffic doubled after the incident.

When MIT Won the Harvard-Yale Game: Hacking Harvard

The supreme authority on MIT hacks—performance and otherwise—is Harvard University. Over the years, the red brick school down the street has been the recipient of more than its fair share. Because it has been hacked so many times—in so many ways—Harvard is an expert on MIT hacks, and the school has its own lore about the way it has been hacked by MIT.

MIT hackers are particularly dedicated to "enhancing" the Ivy League school's most hallowed traditions. It all started in April 1940 when MIT students initiated a series of kidnappings of celebrity guests headed for Harvard. Members of MIT's DKE fraternity, posing as Harvard students, met Eddie Anderson at the Providence airport. The hackers told Anderson, who played Rochester on Jack Benny's radio show, that they were avoiding the crowds at the Boston airport and proceeded to take him to an informal get-together called a smoker at the DKE house at MIT. After awhile, the hackers explained the hoax and transported him to Harvard.

A retaliatory "war" between the two schools ensued over the next two nights with MIT students claiming as their spoils 22.5 pairs of trousers, a belt, and a pair of undershorts. The next night Harvard thought they'd foil any further kidnapping attempts by setting a car and driver out in front of the Metropolitan Theater to transport Anderson to a reception. Alas, the DKE brothers went backstage, escorted him to a waiting car at another entrance, and drove him to his scheduled event, infuriating the Harvard students.

The next year, an MIT hacker posing as a Harvard student picked up burlesque queen Sally Rand after a performance in the Latin Quarter. She was scheduled to entertain at the Harvard freshman smoker but instead was whisked to MIT where she was honored with a reception and the title, "Associate Professor of Entertainment Engineering." Rand was eventually delivered to Harvard and noted that it was the nicest kidnapping she could ever remember. Later that same evening, Tech students escorted the popular French chanteuse Yvette to MIT's Chi Phi fraternity house. After serenading the fraternity she was returned to her rightful engagement at Harvard.

In 1990, Harvard launched a new annual tradition, and MIT was there to celebrate. According to the new custom, an 11 × 20-inch silver platter called "The Yard Plate," would be hidden in Harvard Yard and frosh given the task of locating it. Alas, the MIT "Mole Hole" hacking group found the plate first and delivered it to MIT President Paul Gray's office. Like a baby left on a doorstep, it came complete with note:

We give you this small token in appreciation
of your years of dedication to our traditional Tech values.

We hope you enjoy having this little bit of their tradition.
It might amuse you to know that the Harvard Class of '94
spends an evening searching Harvard Yard
for what is now in your hands...
Please feel free to dispose of the gift as you see fit.

President Gray promptly assembled a delegation of Institute luminaries and, in full academic regalia, they returned the icon to Harvard so that the new tradition could launch on schedule.

Over the years, MIT hackers have been especially keen on hacking the venerable Harvard-Yale football game. In 1940, they burned the letters MIT into the Crimson turf. The Harvard team considered it a jinx and lost the game. Consequently, Crimson officials made certain MIT hackers' attempts were stymied for the next 40-odd years.

In 1948, eight MIT hackers planted primer cord, an explosive used to ignite dynamite, under the turf of the Harvard football field. When set off, it would have burned three huge letters out of the turf—"MIT." A groundskeeper discovered the ends of the wire hidden under the grandstand, however, and removed the cord but left the exposed ends in place to trap the hackers.

On the day of the big game, Harvard authorities spotted a student lurking near the wires attempting to conceal dry cells under his jacket. Apprehended, the hacker explained that "all Tech men carry batteries for emergencies." In tribute, many MIT students wore batteries under their jackets throughout the next week. Boston newspapers reported that the explosives would have blown a crater in the field, but tests performed during the planning stages of the hack showed that the primer cord would have left only a shallow turf burn.

EXAMINING BLAST BATTERIES—Patrolman Peter A. Coletta and Harold J. Finan at Station 14.

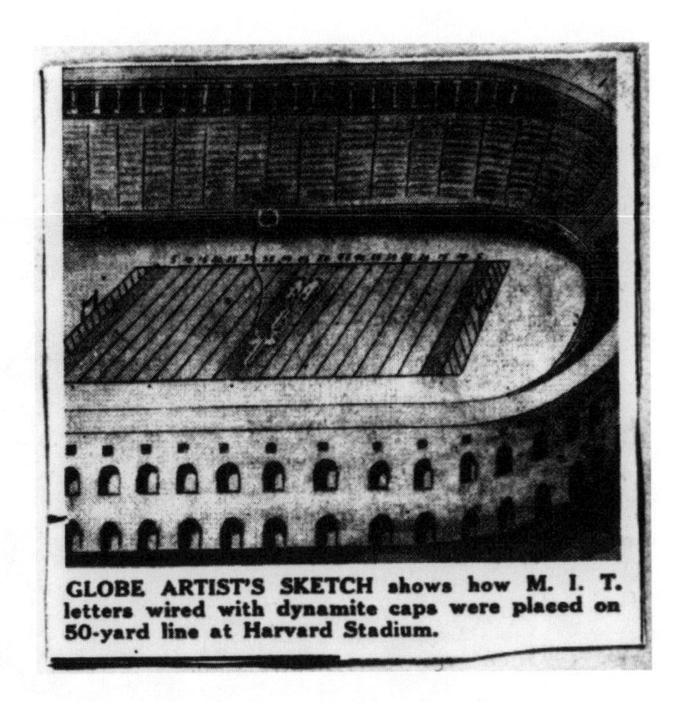

GLOBE ARTIST'S SKETCH shows how M. I. T. letters wired with dynamite caps were placed on 50-yard line at Harvard Stadium.

In 1978, just a few days before the game, Yale students were caught in the act of burning a large "Y" into the field. While repairing the turf, the Harvard grounds crew discovered a remote control spray-painting mechanism under the field. When triggered, the device would have painted towering initials of Harvard's nemesis on the field—"MIT."

It wasn't until 1982 that MIT was again successful at hacking the Harvard-Yale Game, pulling off three legendary hacks in one afternoon. Harvard had not scored against Yale since 1979, but now, with 7:45 minutes remaining in the second period, it had just chalked up its second touchdown. The atmosphere in the stadium was charged. Suddenly a weather balloon burst from the turf at the 46-yard line. As it inflated to six feet, the spectators in Harvard Stadium were just able to make out the oversized white letters that spelled "MIT" before the black balloon burst in a cloud of talcum powder. This hack was the first of three MIT plays.

71

Wearing the signature white pants and sweatshirts of the Yale Marching Band, the forty or so students comprising the MIT Band made it past security guards before the start of the game. At half time, they paraded onto the playing field, stretched out in careful formation and, with their prone bodies, spelled out the letters "MIT."

Cementing their win, hackers passed out cards in the bleachers during the last quarter, telling Harvard fans that, en masse, they would spell "Beat Yale!" On cue, all 1,134 spectators raised their cards—realizing too late, alas, that they spelled "MIT." Few people who attended that game could tell you today whether Harvard or Yale had scored more touchdowns, but they have never forgotten the team that "won" the game. "I thought it was fabulous," said Los Angeles Dodger first baseman Steve Garvey, who happened to be in the stands. "We never had anything like that at the Michigan–Michigan State game" (*Boston Herald American* Nov. 21, 1982).

While this hacking hat-trick was definitely a coup for MIT, the three hacks actually were not a coordinated effort but instead the work of three independent hacking groups that had coincidentally set their sights on the same target.

In 1990, Harvard campus police were lying in wait in the days leading up to the Harvard-Yale game, but this did not deter hackers from MIT's Zeta Beta Tau fraternity. Their aim was to send a rocket-powered banner over the Harvard goal post during the big game, and a little police presence was not going to deter them.

With exceptional perseverance, the hackers soldiered on, even after Harvard police discovered and removed the apparatus, which had been concealed under sod at the zero yard line. From that point on, a row of police cars kept a vigil, their headlights trained on the field after dark. The hackers timed their reinstallation between police shifts, taking care not to leave footprints. This time, they used butter knives to bury the wire that ran from the rocket, under the field, and into the bleachers.

Because they could not test the apparatus on the field, they devised a back-up method. They placed a multimeter between metal bleachers to complete the circuit, then checked for resistance between the two bleachers. If the multimeter read 3 ohms, they knew the hack would go according to plan.

On game day, one of the hackers connected the wires to the battery pack he was wearing in the inner pocket of his jacket, then launched the model rocket engine across the playing field and over the goal post, trailing a banner that read "MIT." As they had in 1982, local newspapers proclaimed

MIT the winner of the game and the Zeta Beta Tau hackers had the satisfaction of demonstrating just why "all Tech men carry batteries."

In 1995, hackers observed the big-game-hacking tradition with a memento set in cement. When MIT poured a new sidewalk, they implanted a bronze relief of a beaver gnawing a Harvard goal post. Claiming a flaw in the cement, the MIT administration removed the panel and replaced it, weeks later, without the embellishment.

Not content to dominate the playing field, hackers in 1982 actually made an attempt to take over Harvard—peacefully and bureaucratically, of course. MIT student government intelligence had revealed that Harvard's student government was in the throes of reorganization. The MIT regime saw this as an excellent opportunity for a hack. They passed a resolution granting Harvard colonial status and appointed an MIT student colonial governor (see Student Leaders at MIT Claim Harvard as Colony). But there were repercussions. During the MIT Undergraduate Association president's speech at the first-year's picnic the next fall, the MIT hacking group "Commando Hacks" staged his abduction. Other members of the hacking team unfurled the banner "Free Harvard." Finally, a ransom note was presented to MIT president Paul Gray demanding that Harvard be released from MIT's tyrannical rule.

Finally, no survey of Harvard hacks is complete without discussion of the Harvard Bridge. Nicknamed the Mass. Ave. Bridge, the Harvard Bridge is a primary vehicular and pedestrian thoroughfare connecting Boston and Cambridge. Back Bay sits on the Boston side, MIT on the Cambridge side. The Harvard campus is located several miles further down Massachusetts Avenue on the Cambridge side.

The reason for this anomaly is history. When the Harvard Bridge was dedicated in 1891, MIT was not located on the bank along the Charles River but in the middle of Back Bay in Boston. The bridge-naming controversy began in 1916 as soon as the MIT campus moved to Boston, and it has continued ever after. On several occasions, when the bridge has been closed for renovations, proposals have been submitted to rename the bridge for MIT. Many at the Institute have considered the span an embarrassing example of civil engineering and have not wanted MIT associated with it. They, at least, have been pleased when name-change attempts have failed to make it through bureaucratic channels.

Hackers, on the other hand, have always felt the Harvard Bridge moniker was a wrong that needed to be righted. They have hacked the bridge a half-dozen times and left MIT's indelible mark with "Smoots" (see The Numbers Game). In 1949, when the bridge was closed for renovations, they changed the "Harvard Bridge Closed" sign to "Technology Bridge Closed." When the bridge opened later that year, the governor of Massachusetts was about to lead a motorcade over it when a convertible cut in front, replacing the official car at the head of the procession. The renegade car carried two clowns, a brass band, and ten members of *The Tech* newspaper staff wielding a sign that read, "The Tech Dedicates Technology Bridge." State police intervened at the last moment, unfortunately, and waved the governor's car ahead, so *The Tech* car was ultimately the second to cross the bridge.

Student Leaders at MIT Claim Harvard as Colony

Jessica Marshall

MIT's colonization of Harvard was described in detail by the "colonists" themselves in the Harvard Crimson.

Anyone who wonders just where to find the center of student authority at Harvard can now look to MIT. Confronted with rumors that Harvard currently lacks a cohesive student government, the MIT Undergraduate Association last Thursday passed a resolution granting Harvard College colonial status and appointing sophomore Paula J. Van Lare colonial governor.

Van Lare said yesterday she does not expect any organized resistance from her new subjects. "Seeing the success Harvard has had organizing itself in the past, I sort of doubt it," she said.

MIT junior Kenneth H. Segel, president of the MIT student government, said yesterday giving Harvard colony status will be no problem, explaining that "basically everything can be reduced to an engineering problem." He added, "We'll probably let you move up to province status if you're good."

[Harvard] Dean of Students Archie C. Epps yesterday expressed surprise at the MIT takeover, saying, "I didn't realize that they learned anything about American government at MIT."

And associate professor of history Bradford Lee questioned the prudence of the move, observing that the invocation of colonial status "usually breeds an anti-colonial movement."

Confirming Lee's prediction, Andrew B. Herrmann ('82)—former chairman of Harvard's Student Assembly—called for a "26-mile blockade around Harvard Square." Asked Herrmann, "What are they going to attack us with—calculators and slide rules? They don't even have a football team."

Harvard's new rulers include the leaders of the MIT Undergraduate Assembly elected in early March. Segel and his running mate, vice-president Kenneth J. Meltsner, also a junior, ran on the Gumby Party, whose motto is "Reason as a Last Resort." After their election, they found that the MIT student body "pretty much had their stuff together" and turned their sights to Harvard.

Besides governor Van Lare, the protectorate also includes sophomore William B. Coney, as secretary of defense, and Deren Hansen, as ambassador to extraterrestrial civilizations. Van Lare said she expects to create other posts for her MIT friends.

Harvard's current Student Assembly chairman Natasha Pearl ('83), when informed that her powers had been usurped, dismissed MIT's gesture of munificence, saying that her own unfunded government doesn't "want their sympathy, just their cash or personal checks."

The John Harvard Hacks

MIT hackers long have had a penchant for pranks on Harvard icons and traditions. The bronze statue of the college's founding father, John Harvard, has proved an irresistible target over the years. Designed, ironically, by MIT alumnus Daniel Chester French, the statue has presided over Harvard Yard for more than a century.

John Harvard's Porto-Potty Service, 1960

Hackers position a toilet stall door in front of the statue along with the advertisement, "Johnny on-the-Spot, Portable Toilets, Rented/Serviced, Boston, Mass. Capital 7–0777."

John Harvard's Brass Rat, 1979

John Harvard proudly sports a Class of 1980 "brass rat," the MIT school ring. To avoid damaging the statue, hackers cast the bronze ring in two parts scaled to the statue's proportions and then use epoxy to join the two halves on the statue's finger.

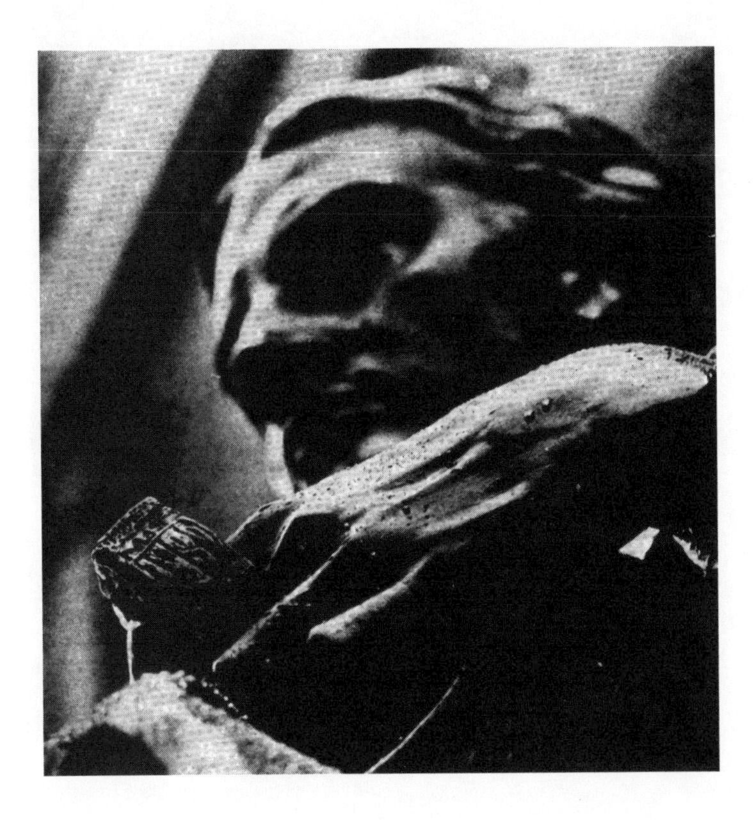

John Harvard's Bad Leg, 1990

To underline the trouncing that both MIT and Yale have just given Harvard at the Harvard/Yale game, MIT hackers place a cast on the statue's right leg, a skull cap on its head, and a regulation MIT Medical Department brace around its neck accessorized with a pin that reads "Ask Me about My Lobotomy."

John Harvard's Visit from Santa, 1996

This John Harvard hack actually took place at MIT. Hackers placed a sack of coal at the bottom of a stairwell. Positioned above it was the red-suited arm of Santa Claus, who had apparently just dropped the bag. The sack was addressed, "To John Harvard. From: Santa Claus. You've been a baaaad boy, Johnny!!"

John Harvard, Unibomber, 1996

When it turns out that Unibomber Ted Kaczynski is a 1962 Harvard graduate, MIT hackers dress up John Harvard to fit the FBI mug shot of Kaczynski that's been distributed in the media—complete with white hooded sweatshirt, unruly hair, moustache, and sunglasses. He also sports a pair of handcuffs.

Often, when a prominent fixture emerges on the campus landscape, members of the MIT community will say, "Well, it's just a matter of time." And everybody knows what that means. The statue, the sign, the vacant lot is just asking to be hacked.

When an information booth called "The Source" was set up in the Student Center in the mid-1990s, hackers had no choice but to set up a spoof booth a few yards away. The sign for "The Sink" looked nearly identical to that of the neighboring booth, but the personnel staffing "The Sink" dressed entirely in black, wore dark glasses, and looked furtively about them as they attempted to collect information from passers-by.

Elevators at MIT are another obvious target, although usually they are hacked for utilitarian purposes—to reach a forbidden floor, for example. In fall 2000, however, hackers transformed both sets of elevators in the student center from mindless machines to erudite and sometimes sarcastic cybervators. When a rider pressed a floor number, the "cybervator" would give a summary of what might be found there, sometimes with biting commentary.

Those pressing the basement button might hear a message saying, "Video arcade, post office, bowling alley," or "There's a basement? Who knew?" If they chose floor one, the elevator might warn, "expensive groceries, expensive banking, expensive clothing, expensive food." On two: "black leather, twisted art, and pango-pango wood." In all there were twelve different messages. Rumor has it that when a campus police officer entered an elevator to investigate, he was warned off, "This is not the hack you're looking for."

Earlier that year, hackers were inspired by another utilitarian machine, the ice cream vending machine in Lobby 16. When a customer selected an item, a large suction arm—similar to that on a vacuum cleaner—would select the product from the freezer and deposit it into the vending slot. This mechanism reminded hackers just a little too much of the aliens in the movie *Toy Story*, who worship "The Claw" that delivers them to waiting children. They placed little green *Toy Story* aliens inside the machine along with the sign:

The vacuum is our master!
The vacuum chooses who will go
and who will stay!

In fact, hackers have often employed animated characters in the service of their creations. When a series of renovations and additions left an inexplicable wall at the bottom of a stairwell in Building 9, hackers propelled the

beleaguered Warner Brothers' critter Wile E. Coyote smack into the dead-end. The hack was actually two clever murals—one of Wile's outline as he tried to pass through the tunnel and another, on a side wall, of the empty box for his ineffectual "Acme Instant Tunnel Kit." The murals still adorn the walls, perhaps as a precaution to unsuspecting pedestrians.

Another cartoon character, the "Grumpy Fuzzball," had its origins at MIT. The fuzzy, heavy-lidded critter appeared at the height of final exams in 1989 when he replaced the owl icon on signs for the Athena network, the central computer system at the Institute. He even replaced the icon on the log-on screen. Athena staff frantically worked to decipher the code to erase him, but the fuzzball spontaneously reverted back to his wise old self the next morning, just as hackers had planned.

In 1978, the hacking group James E. Tetazoo kidnapped the life-size cardboard cartoon Renaissance Man who served as the IAP mascot. IAP, the Independent Activities Period, is an interval between the fall and spring semesters when members of the MIT community can take short courses in everything from wine tasting to boat building. The cartoon mascot outside the IAP office appeared to be doing a little of everything—that is, until he was kidnapped by hackers, who left a photograph and ransom note at the scene. The photo showed him bound, gagged, and being hauled off by a hooded kidnapper. A copy of the *Boston Globe* was propped in the upper right-hand corner of the frame to establish the date.

In their ransom note, hackers made a variety of demands, including that the drop date for courses be extended to sixteen weeks, that all Institute courses be taught in the computer programming language COBOL, and that light observe the 55-mph speed limit. As requested, administrators replied to the kidnappers' demands in *Tech Talk*, the official campus newspaper. In an open letter to the mascot's abductors, they agreed to many of their stipulations. They thought, for example, that slowing down light might be a boon for physicists trying to study it. But they rejected two of the demands: "People can teach classes at MIT in whatever color they choose. As for the 16-week drop date, it simply doesn't go far enough."

Another character who lives large in the MIT mythology is the Squanch, the mascot of East Campus. The Squanch has had many incarnations over the years, and in December 2000 Tetazoo designed a garden in its image. The physicists working in the buildings overlooking the Squanch garden, which is enclosed by buildings 2, 4, and 6, decided they liked the new landscaping just fine, and it has never been disturbed.

We have THE IAP man.
HE will die unless these
demands are met by midnight
the last day of iap:
* iap will be extended 30
days
* the letter "Q" will be
stricken from the alphabet
* all Institute courses shall
be taught in the furlong stone
Fortnigt fsf system
* all classes will be taught in
cobol
* 16th week drop date
* President Wiesner must eat a

lunch at lobdell

* light must observe the 55 mph limit.

WE will Be awaiting reply in tech talk.

After a century of hacking, the entire campus has become infected with the spirit. Staff, administrators, even temporary construction workers get into the act from time to time. In honor of Halloween, workers renovating the MIT Press Bookstore building in 1992, inspired by previous pumpkin hacks and by a multi-story orange tarp that wrapped the site, turned the building into a four-sided, grinning jack-o-lantern.

Another legendary non-student hack was the 1982 "Building Cozy" hack. While perusing the book "Items from Our Catalog," a spoof on the L. L. Bean catalog, Institute real estate officer Philip Trussell was struck with the hacking bug. He submitted a purchase order to Avon Books, publisher of the parody, for Item #6RMS RIVVW, a building cozy, to protect the 23-story Green Building. When the cozy did not arrive, there ensued a correspondence between the MIT "hacker" and the publisher of the fake catalog (see Hacking by Mail).

The employees of the Real Estate Office had been enjoying this joke between their boss and the mock catalog company when, a few weeks later, a large flatbed truck pulled up out front. *Nearly* everyone in the office was flabbergasted to discover that the truck was hauling a massive crate labeled "Building Cozy."

Hacking by Mail

Bitten with the hacking bug, real estate officer Philip A. Trussell attempts to order a "building cozy" from a parody mail-order catalogue.

December 17, 1982

Gentlemen:

A month ago we forwarded to you our purchase order #ES437192 for a building cozy for our Earth Sciences building: color—red check.

We have not received confirmation of our order; however, if the shipment is in the mail (or possibly on a Conrail car), we will forward our check in the amount of $51,575.25 as soon as the order is received.

Thank you for your attention to this matter, and we wish you best wishes for a successful holiday season!

Sincerely,

Philip A. Trussell

January 10, 1983

Dear Mister Trussell:

We are in receipt of your order for Item #6RMS RiVVW, Building Cozy, Red Check model. Unfortunately, we have just received a similar order from the Port Authority of New York and New Jersey. Since this will undoubtedly consume the entire supply of good, honest American red-checked gingham that we might possibly import from Hong Kong over the next few years—to say nothing of the entire East Coast supply of seamstresses and seamsters—I am afraid that we will not be able to guarantee delivery of your order before the next ice age cometh.

In the meantime, perhaps you should consider individual orders of the Solar Watch Cap, which is sturdy enough to warm the most professorial brain.

Yours sincerely,

Ann C. McKeown
Publicity Manager

Zen and the Art of Hacking: The Essays

The following essays are the work of hackers, hackees, students, alumni, and administrators—even Institute President Charles Vest has weighed in. The common denominator is a first-person perspective on the art and science of hacking. The authors' philosophies and anecdotes serve to illustrate why, generation after generation, regardless of changes in trends and mores, hacking continues to thrive at MIT.

The Case of the Disappearing President's Office

MIT President Charles M. Vest

It simply isn't even close when it comes to naming my favorite and most unforgettable hack. That's because I was the hackee.

It all goes back to my very first day on the job nearly twelve years ago, on Monday, October 15, 1990. The late vice president Constantine Simonides was escorting me to my office—his was across the hall—on the second floor of Building 3. When we arrived, however, there was no office to be seen, only a large bulletin board, flush against the wall and covered with newspaper clippings, including several about the search that lead to my selection as president, and also clips from *The Tech* headlines, "Vest Takes over on Monday."

So good was the ruse that Constantine became momentarily disoriented and thought we had, perhaps, while engrossed in conversation, climbed the stairs to the wrong floor.

Then we broke out in hearty laughter when we realized what had happened: the bulletin board, ingeniously constructed and snugly fitted within the opening, was moved aside and, lo, there were the outer doors to the president's and provost's offices.

We gave the bulletin board a place of honor and humor for a time, and I still have it. As I explained later that day to a group I was addressing, "My first major policy is that we're going to keep that. The first time issues get hot on campus, we'll put it back in place." Well, there have been some fairly hot issues, but none so bad that I've had to hide behind the bulletin board.

If there was a message in all this, I suppose, it was that MIT presidents come and go, as do students, but the rich culture and traditions of the Institute will endure. The student hackers, who remained anonymous, left behind a bottle of champagne as a gesture of welcome and goodwill. Later, when we opened it, we toasted the hackers and MIT students generally, whose ever-inventive minds help to make MIT such a special place.

Door Man

Richard Feynman

The first documented hacking group at MIT, the Dorm Goblin transformed the MIT landscape in the 1920s, luring cows to the tops of tall buildings and threading telephone poles through corridors. Although it more than likely happened sporadically beforehand, the Goblin may also be credited with the official launch of door hacking at MIT. In his autobiography Surely You're Joking, Mr. Feynman! *Richard Feynman ('39) recounts his experiences with door hacking. A Nobel Prize-winning physicist, Feynman was equally famous for his practical jokes.*

My masterpiece of mischief happened at the fraternity [Phi Beta Delta]. One morning I woke up very early, about five o'clock, and couldn't go back to sleep, so I went downstairs from the sleeping rooms and discovered some signs hanging on strings which said things like "Door Door! Who Stole the Door?" I saw that someone had taken a door off its hinges, and in its place they hung a sign that said, "Please Close the Door!"—the sign that used to be on the door that was missing.

I immediately figured out what the idea was. In that room a guy named Pete...and a couple of other guys liked to work very hard, and always wanted it quiet. If you wandered into their room looking for something, or to ask them how they did problem such and such, when you would leave you would always hear these guys scream, "Please close the door!"

Somebody had gotten tired of this, no doubt, and had taken the door off. Now this room, it so happened, had two doors, the way it was built, so I got an idea: I took the other door off its hinges, carried it downstairs, and hid it in the basement behind the oil tank. Then I quietly went back upstairs and went to bed.

Later in the morning, I made believe I woke up and came downstairs a little late. The other guys were milling around, and Pete and his friends were all upset. The doors to their room were missing, and they had to study, blah, blah, blah, blah. I was coming down the stairs and they said, "Feynman! Did you take the doors?"

"Oh, yeah!" I said. "I took the door. You can see the scratches on my knuckles here that I got when my hands scraped against the wall as I was carrying it down to the basement.

They weren't satisfied with my answer; in fact, they didn't believe me.

The guys who took the first door had left so many clues—the handwriting on the signs, for instance—that they were soon found out....

The other door stayed missing for a whole week, and it became more and more important to the guys who were trying to study in that room that the other door be found.

Finally, in order to solve the problem, the president of the fraternity says at the dinner table, "We have to solve this problem of the other door. I haven't been able to solve the problem myself, so I would like suggestions from the rest of you as to how to straighten this out, because Pete and the others are trying to study."

Somebody makes a suggestion, then someone else. After a little while, I get up and make a suggestion. "All right," I say in a sarcastic voice, "whoever you are who stole the door, we know you're wonderful. You're so clever! We can't figure out who you are, so you must be some sort of super-genius. You don't have to tell us who you are; all we want to know is where the door is. So if you will leave a note somewhere, telling us where the door is, we will honor you and admit forever that you are a super-marvel, that you are so smart that you could take the other door without our being able to figure out who you are. But for God's sake, just leave the note somewhere, and we will be forever grateful to you for it."

The next guy makes his suggestion: "I have another idea," he says. "I think that you, as president, should ask each man on his word of honor towards the fraternity to say whether he took the door or not."

The president says, "That's a very good idea. On the fraternity word of honor!" So he goes around the table and asks each guy, one by one, "Jack, did you take the door?"

"No sir. I did not take the door."

"Tim, did you take the door?"

"No, sir! I did not take the door."

"Maurice. Did you take the door?"

"No, I did not take the door, sir."

"Feynman, did you take the door?"

"Yeah, I took the door."

"Cut it out, Feynman; this is serious! Sam! Did you take the door..."—it went all the way around. Everyone was shocked. There must be some real rat in the fraternity who didn't respect the fraternity word of honor!

That night, I left a note with a little picture of the oil tank and the door next to it, and the next day they found the door and put it back.

Sometime later I finally admitted to taking the other door, and I was accused by everybody of lying. They couldn't remember what I had said. All they could remember was their conclusion after the president of the fraternity had gone around the table and asked everybody, that nobody admitted taking the door. The idea they remembered, but not the words.

People often think I'm a faker, but I'm usually honest, in a certain way—in such a way that often nobody believes me!

It's Not a Job, It's an Adventure
David Barber

As the Confined Space Program Coordinator at MIT, I and my partner Gary Cunha, evaluate, manage, and remove hacks at the Institute. To the best of my knowledge, we're the only people at MIT—maybe the only two people *anywhere*—whose job descriptions include "hack management." This unusual duty has given us a special perspective on hacks and the people who perform them.

Whenever a hack appears on campus, Gary and I are asked to come up with a game plan for either allowing the hack to remain or for immediate removal. Here are the basic criteria we use to determine whether a hack should remain:

1) Safety to the public
2) Damage to any MIT property
3) Potential damage to the environment
4) Changing weather conditions
5) Resources necessary for removal
6) Whether the hack was "expected"

Sometimes the hackers contact me directly to inform me of their latest creation. These communications usually arrive overnight, often in the form of anonymous e-mail messages that alert me to the installation of the hack, give its reasons for being, and request a specified stay of execution. Occasionally, the hackers' method of communicating with me can cause almost as much commotion as the hack itself. I recall once when the communication was left in a cardboard box by my office complex and someone mistook it for an incendiary device.

The hackers may also provide me with the details of how they put the hack together, a description of the precautions they have taken to protect the community and the property, and instructions on how to disassemble the hack in the safest and most efficient manner. In the midst of the removal process, we often find little surprises, an edible treat, for example, to provide us with a smile as we undertake our duties.

Perhaps our most famous—and certainly best attended—removal, with more than 300 people on hand, was the dismantling of the frieze in the lobby of Building 7. Hackers had "edited" the wording of the Institute credo to read "Established for Advancement and Development of Science its Application to Industry the Arts *Entertainment and Hacking.*" This hack was the most ingenious we'd ever removed. The texture of the materials used, the match of the coloration to the existing inscription, the carving of the letters, and the placement of the frieze were of a caliber befitting the best traditions of hacking at MIT.

In fact, this hack was installed so skillfully that, unless you were looking for it, you probably would not have known it was there. It was in place for two days before anybody noticed it—a testament to the quality of the hackers' craftsmanship and their attention to detail. The hackers also exhibited elaborate care to ensure that they did not damage the installation's surroundings and graciously provided MIT's director of facilities Victoria Sirianni with an anonymous note detailing how the frieze was constructed and how it could be removed without damaging the building.

Communicating with the hacking community has been one of the more interesting facets of my job over the years. At one point, I was approached by a journalist who was interested in writing an article about hacks in general and MIT hacks in particular. The journalist and I had several conversations relative to the MIT tradition of hacks and the hacking community. This person then asked if it would be possible to get an interview with a current member of MIT's hacking community. I posed this question to some people I believed had access to the hackers. Eventually, I got a blind conversation going with a group of the hackers about this possibility. The journalist wanted to interview anonymously, stressing that no names would be used, and offered to provide aliases for the hackers who were interviewed. After several rounds of parallel conversations, it was decided that the journalist would ask me the questions via e-mail and I would relay them to the hackers. The hackers would then send the answers back to me and I would forward the answers to the journalist, after removing all references to the hackers' identities from the electronic correspondence. The magazine got its article and the hackers' identities remained secret. In fact, I still don't know the identities of the people with whom I was in contact.

Inevitably, the hackers eventually decided to hack the hack removal team itself. My hacking response team, the Confined Space Rescue Team (CSRT), carried our rescue equipment in a converted ambulance. Whenever we were in the midst of "hack removal" activities, our vehicle would be parked nearby, so it came to be synonymous with the CSRT. One morning we discovered that our response vehicle had been transformed into a "Hackbusters" mobile. The hackers had adorned our converted ambulance with clear appliqués (one- to two-feet tall, and several feet in length) identifying it as the "Official Hackbuster" vehicle in the style of the vehicle used in the *Ghostbusters* movies. "Hack" was circled in red and had a diagonal line crossed through it. True to the attention to detail that hackers are famous for, the Hackbusters hack came complete with a note to us that included instructions on how to best remove the decals. The note even informed us about the make-up of the materials used in the hack, explaining that they were safe and would not harm the paint on the vehicle.

Historically, the Great Dome has been the number-one target for hacks. Over the years, it has been adorned with a piano, a barbell weight, and of course the infamous police car. I have also seen it transformed into a variety of forms, including a giant beanie cap. On that occasion, hackers draped the dome with red dyed-silk parachute material cut into strips to

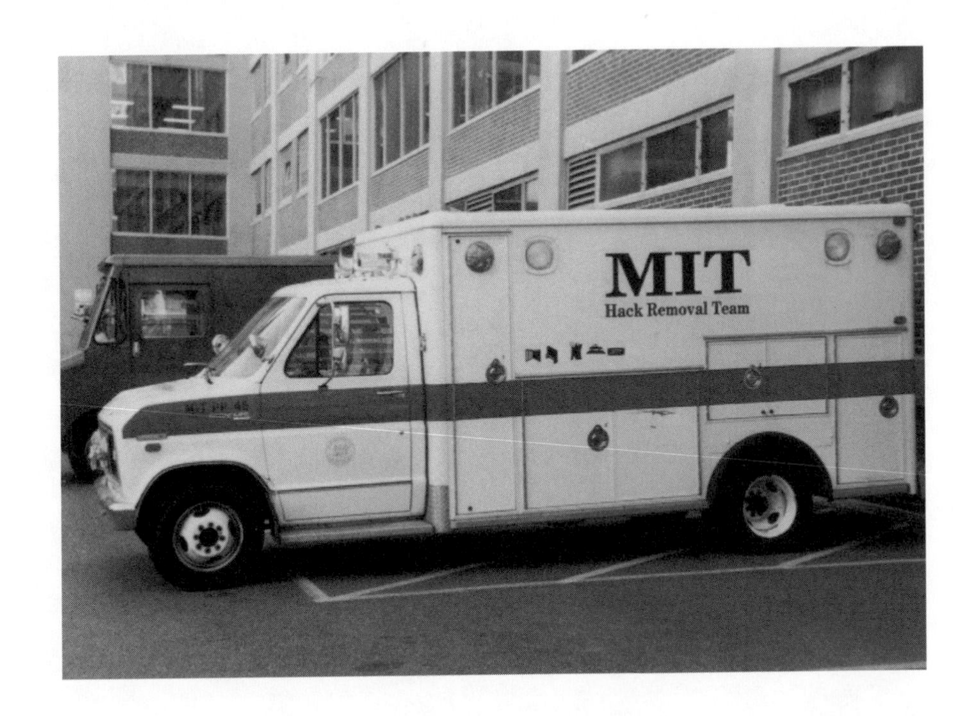
MIT
Hack Removal Team

Ha
IHTFP

create the visual effect of a striped beanie cap and topped it with a propeller with 28-foot long blades that were so perfectly balanced, they rotated in the wind. Most recently, the dome sported the gold ring from *The Lord of the Rings,* complete with authentic inscription. This particular hack came complete with a "hack-back" guarantee: if we would leave the hack in place up through the opening date of the movie, then the hackers would remove the hack. We did and they did.

Some years hackers are more prolific than others. One year, for example, we had four hacks in the course of a single week: a tribute to Douglas Adams, the "Magic Pi Ball" on Building 54, a dinghy in the moat of the MIT Chapel, and the barbell weight on the top of the Great Dome.

As MIT's official hack removal team, we wait and wonder what will be placed on the Great Dome next or what remarkable transformation will occur somewhere else on campus. We also speculate about how hackers will be inspired by some of the new buildings under construction at MIT. Will it be the new dormitory on Vassar Street or the Stata Center that is christened first with the results of the hackers' ingenuity?

With the symbiotic relationship between MIT and the hackers, it seems only fitting that some space be found where historic hacks can have a permanent home, a place that is worthy of their contribution toward making MIT the most interesting place to work in the world.

The Great Breast of Knowledge
Brian Leibowitz

In his 1990 Journal of the Institute for Hacks, TomFoolery & Pranks at MIT, *Brian Leibowitz gives a behind-the-scenes account of the design and creation of the "The Great Breast of Knowledge" hack—a case study in the skills and perseverance necessary to execute a hack on the Institute's Great Dome. Here is an excerpt.*

The notion that the Great Dome resembles a giant breast was first suggested in the living group Burton One in December 1978. During IAP (Independent Activities Period) in January 1979, blueprints of the dome were studied and the proper dimensions for the nipple and aureole were determined. The nipple was then constructed using a wooden frame covered with chicken wire and pink paper.

As hackers prepared to haul it up the side of the building, campus police came upon the nipple sitting on the roof of the hackers' car. Undaunted by this setback, the group planned their second attempt. This time, practice sessions were held to hone climbing skills and to reduce the time needed to transfer the nipple from the car to the roof. Alas, preparations notwithstanding, implementation was foiled again—the hackers were spotted by a cleaning woman, so they decided to postpone the hack.

Alleged treachery barred the Burton group's third attempt, when campus police, acting on an anonymous tip, arrived at the scene to stop what they had been led to believe was a robbery in progress. Their escape hampered by a snagged rope, two members of the hacker roof crew were caught. After a chat with the campus police chief, the students agreed not to try again that semester. Later learning that the anonymous tipster may have been a student from another floor of their own dorm, the hackers realized that secrecy was now essential to their success.

The annual freshman picnic marked the beginning of a new semester, and a new plan was formed. A redesigned, collapsible nipple did not have to be brought up the side of the building, but could be carried in backpacks. On this, their fourth attempt, the Burton hackers announced to their dormitory that the project had been called off. Finally, during the freshman picnic, the Burton One Outdoor Breast Society successfully installed the Great Breast of Knowledge with its accompanying banner, "Mamma Maxima Scientiae."

Mastery over the Physical World: Demonstrative and Pedagogical Value of the MIT Hack

André DeHon

I've always enjoyed a good hack, so as a freshman entering MIT, I was delighted to get my first-choice housing selection. It meant I would be able to associate myself with a hall in an MIT dormitory that took as its motto: "Hackito Ergo Sum." I hack, therefore I am.

As a graduate student, and now as an alum, I've made a point of photographing MIT hacks, collecting interesting tidbits, and helping share those with the world—in large part through the IHTFP Gallery, a Web site devoted to MIT hacks, http://hacks.mit.edu. From time to time people ask me why a busy alum bothers to spend time documenting hacks. The answer lies in understanding the relationship of hacking to MIT.

Hacking, while playful and irreverent on the surface, is really very much about MIT's value system. Hacking, perhaps more than anything else, gives the world a glimpse into the complex ecosystem that makes MIT such a special environment. To use another metaphor, it's like a shard of a hologram—it's not the whole, but it is a piece through which you can see what the whole might be like.

Hacks provide an opportunity to demonstrate creativity and know-how in mastering the physical world. In that respect, they reflect the Institute's value system. At MIT, intellect and its application are valued, as opposed to athletic prowess, for example. So, while other schools get excited about their sporting teams, MIT students eagerly anticipate the annual mechanical engineering design contest. And the next hack. MIT is not about "our jocks beating your jocks" but "our nerds mastering the physical world" by, for example, putting a campus police cruiser on top of a nine-story-tall dome or inflating a balloon in the middle of the field during a Harvard-Yale game. It's not *we can run faster than you*, it's *we can manipulate the physical world to do things you hadn't imagined were possible.* As character Chris Knight says in the 1985 film *Real Genius,* it's about "using your mind creatively."

An important component of many hacks is to help people see something in a different way, to give it a humorous, satirical, or poignant twist. As Eri Izawa notes in Engineering in Action, giving people a jolt out of the intense atmosphere at MIT reminds them to smell the roses and helps put the day-to-day trials into a big-picture perspective. And, of course, the MIT administration occasionally does or proposes some pretty silly things, like putting a giant hairball outside the cafeteria in the student center (see "All Mondays Should Be So Beautiful"). There was a sequence of at least three hacks surrounding the whole hairball controversy, and they helped focus some of the discussion at the time. Fortunately, there was still no hairball in front of the dining facility the last time I visited Cambridge!

Hacks are good show for the outside world, they are good morale boosters for the MIT community, and they really are good for the students involved—whether or not they realize it at the time. It encourages them to think creatively, an essential skill for innovative engineers and scientists, and it gives them experience solving real engineering problems.

MIT hackers thrive on new ways to view old venues (*hmm, Lobby 7 would make a nice cathedral*) or current events (*we need to demonstrate the folly of a giant hairball in front of the cafeteria*). They generate visions of the way the world might be and then turn them into reality—with no artificial constraints, supervision by elders, or safety net. Hacking is an excellent training ground in the small for acquiring the skills and experience necessary to be visionaries and doers in the large. Hacks attack focused problems not circumscribed by grades or artificial rules, but by real-world engineering constraints (costs, difficulty, physical properties of materials, access, politics). They are not judged on effort or conformity but solely by success, impact, and personal satisfaction. These experiences are the key ingredients to nurture excellent engineers, managers, and skunk-work teams.

Yes, classes have their role. It is necessary to know core facts and analysis and get focused experience using this knowledge and these techniques (labs, projects, homework). Classes, however, must be tailored to the large volume of students. Problems must be of a narrow enough scope to be doable by everyone and must have considerable uniformity to be gradable by limited course staff. For this reason, hacks are a real complement to a student's formal classroom and lab training.

In hacking, there is no teaching assistant or professor to bail you out when things don't work...just like in the real world, you have to find a way to solve the problem yourself. This forces you to tackle the whole problem, the whole experience, and it builds confidence and independence. MIT hackers learn to envision new things. They learn management, delegation, teamwork, planning, failure analysis, and public relations. As Izawa writes in her essay, they really get to see "engineering in action" in an open enough setting to be real, and they see this on a timescale short enough to facilitate rapid learning. They learn that they can turn their own visions into reality, and they learn how to do it.

It's hard to imagine a more valuable tradition for an institution like MIT. The fact that this tradition was not handed down by the faculty or administration, but evolved among the students and continues to thrive, is indicative of the special environment that is MIT.

André DeHon spent a decade at MIT (1986–1996) observing MIT hacking culture, during which time he also managed to finish several degrees in electrical engineering and computer science. He is now observing the art of hacking as practiced by the students of MIT's West Coast rival Caltech, where he is an assistant professor of computer science.

Where the Sun Shines, There Hack They

Samuel Jay Keyser

The title of Brian Leibowitz' historical compendium of MIT hacks, *The Journal of the Institute for Hacks, TomFoolery & Pranks at MIT* (MIT Museum, 1990) is itself a hack. Embedded in it are the initials IHTFP, which, as everyone at MIT knows, stand for "I hate this fucking place." This is not the acronym's only "public" commemoration. The Class of 1995 changed the date embossed on the Dome image in the class ring from MCMXVI to IHTFP, something obvious only with a magnifying glass or a sharp eye. Earlier classes have done similar recodings of the MIT ring.

During my years as associate provost for institute life, many of my colleagues approached me with this question: If students hate this place, then why don't they just plain leave it? It is a good question to which, I think, there is a good answer: they DON'T hate this place. But if they don't, the conversation continues, why say they do? An equally good question.

The answer lies, I believe, in unpacking the hacking. When we do, we find the practical joke-cum-parody lurking beneath. The practical joke is physical in character. One does not tell practical jokes. One plays them. Similarly, one does not tell hacks. They, too, are played. Here is how Arthur Koesler describes the practical joke in his *Encyclopedia Britannica* article:

The coarsest type of humour is the practical joke: pulling away the chair from under the dignitary's lowered bottom. The victim is perceived first as a person of consequence, then suddenly as an inert body subject to the laws of physics: authority is debunked by gravity, mind by matter; man is degraded to a mechanism.

The operative words here are "authority debunked." The hack is a physical joke designed to do just this. But it is not any physical joke. Hacks have a strong element of parody in them. They are physical jokes that parody the honest work of an Institute grounded in science and engineering. That is why MIT hacks, unlike hacks at other institutions, always have a strong engineering component. They make fun of engineering by impersonating it and then pulling the seat out from under. MIT hackers typically don't throw pies or wrap underwear around statues of founding fathers. Rather, they make large objects appear in inaccessible places, rewire lecture hall blackboards to go haywire when the instructor tries to use them, replace chiseled wisdom on friezes with silly sayings in what appears to be identical script and then do so so cleverly that it takes a SWAT team of trained rappellers to dismantle them.

Why does MIT hacking have such a long half-life? The answer lies in something called "disobedient dependency." In order to stay in a dependent relationship that is both desirable and yet threatening, one coping mechanism is disobedience. It distances the dependency, makes it bearable. Let me give an example drawn from my experience as a housemaster at Senior House. During the 1980s President Gray and his wife gave garden parties for the parents of incoming freshmen. The President's garden was filled with incoming sons and daughters and their parents. Several Senior House students took this as an opportunity to be ostentatiously disobedient. They would dress as grungily as possible. Then they would scale the wall separating the Senior House courtyard from the President's House garden and mingle with the well-dressed, well scrubbed guests, scarfing crabmeat sandwiches as if they were auditioning for the part of John Belushi in a remake of *Animal House*. The more outrageous the behavior, the better. Some of the more inventive students would dress up as characters from *The Rocky Horror Picture Show.* Most, however, did not, attempting to *épater le bourgeois*, as it were, without props. More often than not, someone would dump a bottle of detergent in the garden fountain in order to intensify the nuisance value of his or her presence.

The superficial motive behind such "disobedience" was to embarrass those in authority, the President, his spouse, the various deans, and housemasters who showed up for the occasion. The crashers were declaring their independence from the Institute and all its folderol. The deeper motive was to provide distance between themselves and the Institute so that its judgments of them, upon which they deeply depended, would be less painful when they were made.

Why do I say that students deeply depend on the Institute's judgments of them? The reason is that the values of the students and of the faculty are the same. For the most part, the faculty are the best at what they do. The students come here to be like them. When the faculty grades them, those judgments can be painful because the students believe they are true. At some level our students know that while they are all in the top five percent of their high school classes, they will soon be recalibrated downward. I say "at some level" because a poll taken not too long ago asked the incoming class how many of them thought they would end up in the top quarter. Something like seventy-five percent said they would! At least half of those responding were about to discover they were not as good as they thought, not an easy pill to swallow at any stage of one's life.

Unlike the extreme kinds of disobedience that one often finds in living groups, the hack is a socially acceptable form of disobedience. It is easily distinguished from its more extreme counterparts by three properties. Hacks are (1) technologically sophisticated, (2) anonymous, (3) benign. They are technologically sophisticated because they need to parody an MIT education. They are anonymous because were they otherwise, the Institute might be forced, if only for safety reasons, to do something about them. They are benign because their goal is not to inflict pain, but to cope with pain inflicted. They do this by making fun of the Institute, diminishing it, bringing it down to size so that its judgments are brought down to size as well.

The hack is a pact that the Institute and its students enter into. Keep it anonymous, harmless, and fun and MIT will look the other way. It will even be mildly encouraging because it recognizes, as do the students, that students need to turn the Institute into an adversary. This, by the way, is why the adversarial undercurrent between students and the Institute won't go away, no matter how supportive student services are or how solicitous our staff might be or how accessible the faculty makes itself.

The hack isn't the only buffering mechanism. Another is the special relationship that students have to their living groups. Why does where a student lives take on such monumental proportions at MIT? Part of the answer is that living groups function much like disobedience; namely, as a kind of protection against the slings and arrows of institutional judgment. Living groups are safe houses, ports in a storm, raingear to keep them dry once the firehose is turned on. This them/us division is so profound, in fact, that long after they have graduated, students talk in terms not of having been at MIT but rather of having been at Senior House, or Sigma Chi, or MacGregor. MIT tacitly acknowledges this as well, which is why changing the very peculiar system of residence selection called R/O is like pulling teeth. The buffering function of the resident system is as much a part of an MIT education as are the General Institute Requirements. The same is true of hacks.

Hacks and living groups, then, are to the Institute what sunglasses are to the sun: a form of protection that makes it possible to live with the light. Not every student hacks. Not every student feels the same degree of disobedient dependency. But every time hackers help to place a police car on the dome, they are providing shade in a very sunny clime.

Samuel Jay Keyser is professor emeritus of linguistics and holder of the Peter de Florez chair emeritus at MIT. He was associate provost for institute life from 1986 through 1994 and came by his experience with hacking during those halcyon years and during his tenure as housemaster of Senior House. He returned to his faculty duties in 1994 and retired, exhausted, four years later, though he still serves as special assistant to the chancellor.

Engineering in Action
Eri Izawa

"Hacking" at the Massachusetts Institute of Technology has nothing to do with the popular image of breaking into computer systems. Instead, it is the production of clever and benign pranks meant to amuse and awe the public; in their ideal form, hacks are a melding of art, inspiration, and engineering. Hacks range from the famous campus police cruiser on the Great Dome and the MIT-labeled weather balloon in the 1982 Harvard-Yale game, to less well-known pranks, like the giant slide rule in the Student Center atrium and the Christmas lights that spelled out "MIT" in six-foot-tall letters on the Little Dome. Hacks have become a way of life at MIT; hardly a term goes by without strange objects appearing in odd places.

But as common as hacks have become, they still require a great deal of insight, hard work, and old-fashioned engineering. Although some hackers may not fully realize it at the time, the production of a successful hack follows the same creative and technical process as any large-scale engineering project—with the added complication that, along with traditional issues such as cost, safety, and manageability, hackers must avoid getting caught by the campus police! (Though many hacks happen in public places, some are set up on places such as rooftops, which are not meant for public access.)

The first step of planning any hack is to decide upon the final product. Often, this is the "What if?" stage. The giant Plexiglas® slide rule that appeared in the Student Center, for example, was the work of students who, tired of the plans for an unpopular shaman's hat sculpture made with human hair, decided to construct something more symbolic of MIT's "nerd image," while providing an unobstructed view of the atrium. Hence, they decided to build a slide rule made of transparent Plexiglas®. Of course, sometimes hackers just decide that it's time to "pull a hack" for no particular reason at all.

Hacks must also pass a "couth" (the opposite of "uncouth") test to be considered a true hack, as opposed to an obnoxious and worthless prank. Hacks must be amusing and generally benign. For example, an idea that may be interpreted as racist would be discarded. The making of fake notices of student loan cancellations, which resulted in hysterical phone calls to the Bursar's Office, is a case where the perpetrators failed to apply the couth test. In addition, hacks that cause permanent structural damage are avoided; hackers believe that property damage is not only inappropriate but bad for future hacks, since repair costs could result in an administrative backlash against hackers.

Once the general idea has been established and accepted, the design begins. As with any engineering project, cost is an important initial factor. Funding comes exclusively from hackers' pockets. Since many hackers tend to be undergraduate students, as one anonymous hacker puts it, "they also tend to be poor." For a group of ten hackers, the cost of a hack rarely exceeds $100, or $10 per person, and "anything above $8–10 per person would require the hack to be something really astonishing," says the hacker. To reduce costs, some hackers forage in trash bins and scrap piles of building materials.

Time is also a valued student commodity. Although something as simple as a banner may require more than one hundred hours to make, individual hackers hope to spend no more than ten or twenty hours on construction; most students cannot afford to spend more than a few hours per week. Consequently, larger hacks often require the involvement of many students to spread out the workload, and some hacks may take months to complete. As with any project involving a large number of people, this necessitates careful management, coordination, and planning. Luckily for the hacking process, many students tend to be willing to spend an entire night devoted to deploying a hack, probably because it is far more exciting than construction.

Conscientious hackers, like good engineers, are also concerned about hack safety. A hacker's worst nightmare is seeing a hack fall off a rooftop; aside from the fact that bystanders may be injured, it's an embarrassment. To prevent safety and structural problems, many hacks are deliberately "overbuilt." For example, one hacker says, "The slide rule (thirty-five pounds of Plexiglas®) was held up by eight 300-pound test ropes, each individually tied." Outdoor hacks require special protection against the elements, especially the wind. Banners are often made of cloth, because paper banners have been known to rip in strong winds. Wind also increases the strain on ropes by turning anything with an exposed surface into a sail; hence, the Christmas lights hack had a volleyball net substrate, which has minimal wind resistance, and was tied down with weighted robes and duct tape. Still, unforeseen conditions can ruin a hack: an effort to change the color tiles on the Media Lab building ended prematurely when sunlight warped the painted wooden replacement tiles so much that they fell off; luckily, the tiles were at ground level and posed no safety hazard.

Unlike most engineering projects, hackers have the added worry of trying to make sure they don't get stopped by non-hackers during the final installation. In engineering terms, this simply means that there are tighter-than-usual constraints on portability and the rapid assembly process. Although a hack may soak up more than one hundred hours to build, ideally it should only take a few minutes to "deploy." Hackers are willing (although only grudgingly so) to wait hours for the perfect deployment moment (when no witnesses are present), but they aren't willing to spend hours installing a hack where they can be spotted. The more exposed the area, or the higher the traffic through the area, the more practice and planning is required.

This also means that a hack should be transportable, so that the hackers can quickly bring it out of storage to its intended destination at a moment's notice (ideal conditions tend to be short-lived). Extremely large hacks, such as the campus police cruiser and the two-story screw that graced the Great Dome, must be built modularly so that the parts can fit through doors and be transported to the deployment area. Banners or large nets with objects attached are rolled or folded up.

The need for rapid deployment also means that a hack must have only a few simple, readily accessible attachments to quickly and securely fasten it to the wall, ceiling, or rooftop. Having too many attachments is confusing, time-consuming, and tends to involve lots of ropes that get tangled easily. Anything more complicated than simple clamps, ropes, weights, and knots are avoided as well. The time-honored "KISS engineering principle" (keep it simple, stupid) aptly applies. Of course, a large hack supported at only a few places needs special attention to structural stability.

A final design factor conscientious hackers consider is removability. Good hacks should be removable without causing structural damage or ideally, any damage at all. In fact, most hackers prefer to take down their own hacks, in part to retrieve equipment before it gets confiscated, and in part because they feel that they are most qualified to take their hacks down safely. Hence, means of attaching hacks to a surface are usually limited to non-permanent techniques. This is generally in accordance with rapid-deployment techniques that stress the use of knots and weights instead of time-consuming welding torches or drilling equipment. One example of the importance of removability is the die hack, in which a cloth with dots (like those found on dice) was placed without official permission over an officially permitted large cubic structure hanging in Lobby 7. The hackers later helped both MIT Physical Plant and the creators of the cube take down the fabric safely and easily. Apparently, the hackers were inspired to help when they learned that the plan to remove the hack would have made the fabric even harder to remove than before. The speedy removal was especially important because the cube was to be displayed as part of an important meeting between an MIT research group and Japanese representatives.

Once the design has been finalized, construction begins. Luckily, finding and using construction equipment is rarely a problem. Although most hackers shy away from projects that would require thesis-level complexity, many of them are competent with and have access to power tools, sewing machines, electronics, and shop equipment. Other construction necessities, such as paint and duct tape, are even easier to acquire and use. One of the worst construction issues is space, since hacks tend to be large. "This wouldn't be so bad except hackers also usually don't want people to know there's a hack under construction," notes an anonymous hacker. Most large hacks end up spread out in living group hallways, empty classrooms, or even unused subbasements.

Once constructed, hackers try to test all the parts of the hack to make sure the Christmas lights actually light, to see that banners won't sag, or make sure tape will stick to the wall. As any good engineer knows, the failure to test something may mean finding flaws the hard way. For example, more than one unfortunate group has found that pulling something up the side of a building with a rope doesn't work because the concrete edge of a roof will cut through even thick rope. Also, the hackers need to test their own skills: knot-tying, climbing, and other deployment necessities. Though hackers would love to rehearse the deployment at least once, generally they cannot risk practicing at the actual site and must make do with off-site practices and verbal descriptions of what is to happen.

After design, construction, and testing, a hack is ready to be deployed. With luck, all goes as planned. An example of a fast successful deployment is the attempt to change the tile colors on the Media Lab. From the all-clear starting signal, to the placing of ladders and fake wooden tiles on the wall, to the removal of the last ladder, was a mere three minutes. Another successful deployment took longer: the Christmas lights hack took more than twenty minutes, time mostly spent making sure that a pile of boxes painted as presents were safely glued to each other. According to one hacker, the problem was that they "hadn't taken into account the fact that glues tend to dry more slowly in cold weather." Still, twenty minutes wasn't too bad because, as another hacker put it, "rooftops are relatively low-visibility areas." Of course, the Christmas lights weren't turned on until the hackers were ready to leave.

Assuming the arrival of campus police hasn't halted the deployment prematurely, the hackers do final checks on their hack, and then slip away, leaving MIT, and sometimes the rest of the world, to marvel at their handiwork. Perhaps only fellow hackers, however, can truly appreciate the effort, ingenuity, and planning that has gone into the design, construction, and implementation of the best hacks. It is engineering in action.

Eri Izawa is an MIT physics graduate ('92). She has worked in fields ranging from computer game design, software engineering, Webmastering, art, and writing, to playing useless computer games.

Why We Hack

Anonymous

Why do hackers hack? While the question isn't terribly important to the enjoyment of hacks (you should be paying attention to the hack; please ignore the folks in black scurrying away with ladders and ropes), in a book on hacks the subject might come up. I should be clear up front that I don't presume to speak for all hackers—the hacking community at MIT is as diverse as any other community, and the ideas I present here are far from universal.

Many of us hack first and foremost because it is fun. It's fun to scale tall buildings and plant unusual objects there. It's fun to do difficult things and do them well. It's fun to make people smile, and it's fun to make them scratch their heads in wonder.

Most hacks represent a feat of engineering—sometimes it's electronics or mechanics, and sometimes it's the logistics of getting six people and an eight-foot-tall papier-mâché beaver through the halls of the Institute at 2 a.m. without arousing the suspicion of the campus police or custodial staff. As Samuel Jay Keyser points out, we like to play at engineering (see Where the Sun Shines, There Hack They). I suggest that it's not so much that we play at engineering because we are engineers, but rather we are engineers because we like to play at engineering.

Other hacks are well-timed art, where the beauty is in the elegance of the medium and the appropriateness of the message, coupled with the challenge of deploying the art visibly without official sanction. One thing common to almost every hack is that it involves doing something most people wouldn't think of doing. It should come as no surprise that hacks abound at MIT, a place dedicated to doing things other people haven't thought of doing.

Many hacks involve lost sleep, suffering grades, and the risk of roof fines. The greatest part of an MIT education (in this alum's humble opinion) is the understanding that not all things are of equal importance—some things are more fun than sleep, and sometimes it's worth incurring a roof fine or lower grades to do something worth doing.

How about anonymity? Secrecy helps us do our job, certainly, but there is also a modesty that infuses the engineering tradition. The artist should not get in the way of the art, and the designer should not get in the way of the design. No amount of advertising or cajoling can turn a bad design into a good one; instead you put your work out for public scrutiny and let others evaluate. Anonymity is not without its perks. It's quite a thrill to have someone point out your hack to you as something you *must see*.

Seemingly at odds with the desire for anonymity is the performance hack. Witnesses to the hack can see the perpetrators, and some might even recognize them. Performance hacks require a slightly different mind-set, and tend to be of a different type than engineering hacks. Really, though, in a community of 20,000 people if you can keep your name out of the papers (and history books), it's likely that most of the witnesses will remember the hack and not the person behind it.

A successful hack brings the satisfaction of having brightened the days of many people. An unsuccessful hack teaches valuable principles of engineering—plan ahead and check theory with experiment. What better pastime for aspiring scientists and engineers?

Glossary of MIT Vernacular

10–1000	Unofficial room number of the Great Dome
'93 dorm	Now known as the East Campus dormitory
APO	Alpha Phi Omega, a service fraternity
ATO	Alpha Tau Omega fraternity
Athena	Central MIT computer network
Baker House	Dormitory
Beast from the East	Floor in the East Campus dormitory
Beaver	MIT's mascot
Brass Rat	MIT's school ring ("rat" refers to the beaver on the ring)
Bruno	Unit of measurement resulting from the free fall of a piano (see The Numbers Game)
Burton House	Dormitory
Coffeehouse Club	Informal affiliation of hackers who meet regularly to explore the Institute and share hacking knowledge
DKE or Deke	Delta Kappa Epsilon fraternity
Dome	There are two—"The Great Dome" over Building 10 and a smaller dome over Building 7 (see Domework)

East Campus	Dormitory (originally called the '93 dormitory)
Fishbowl	Located off the Infinite Corridor, historically one of the most visible Athena computer clusters
Great Dome	Larger of the two Institute domes, over Building 10
Hack	An inventive, anonymous prank (see Hack, Hacker, Hacking)
Harvard Bridge	Bridge connecting Boston to Cambridge at MIT
Hell	MIT
Hosed	Overwhelmed with homework
IAP	Independent Activities Period, in January between the fall and spring terms
I.H.T.F.P.	"I Hate This F*&^ing Place" and infinite variations (see Intriguing Hacks to Fascinate People)
IHTFP Gallery	Online gallery of MIT hacks at http://hacks.mit.edu
ILG	Independent living group
Infinite Corridor	Quarter-mile-long corridor cutting through the heart of the Institute
Jack E. Florey	Hacking group from the East Campus dormitory (Fifth East)
James E. Tetazoo	Hacking group from the East Campus dormitory (Third East)
Killian Court	Large courtyard facing the Great Dome on one side and the Charles River on the other

Larry	Archenemy of James Tetazoo and champion of Elvis, this hacking group congregates around the forty-first floor of the western front of East Campus
Lobdell	Cafeteria in the student center
MacGregor House	Dormitory
ORK	Order of Random Knights, a hacking group from the Random Hall dormitory
R/O	Residence and Orientation Week for incoming students
Rush	Period during R/O when new members were recruited for living groups (recruiting was discontinued in 2001)
Senior House	Dormitory
Smoot	Unit of length used to measure the Harvard Bridge (see The Numbers Game)
Squanch	Mascot of Third East in the East Campus dormitory
Tech	MIT (outdated)
The Tech	Student newspaper founded in 1881
Tech Talk	Campus newspaper published by the MIT News Office since 1957
THA	Technology Hackers Association, a now-defunct hacking group and one of the preeminent forces in the annals of hacking
Tool	To study, or one who studies too much

Sources

"Hack, Hacker, Hacking" reprinted from *The Journal of the Institute for Hacks, TomFoolery & Pranks at MIT.* The MIT Museum, 1990.

"Hacking Ethics" reprinted from *Is This the Way to Baker House?* The MIT Museum, 1996.

"Father Tool's Grand Tour" reprinted from *Is This the Way to Baker House?*

"U.S.S. Tetazoo" reprinted from *The Journal of the Institute for Hacks, TomFoolery & Pranks at MIT.*

"No Knife" reprinted from *The Journal of the Institute for Hacks, TomFoolery & Pranks at MIT.*

"Why Ruin the Atrium?" reprinted from *Is This the Way to Baker House?*

"Green Eggs and Hair" reprinted from *Is This the Way to Baker House?*

"A Guide for New Employees: Building History and Numbering System" reprinted from web.mit.edu/development/new.employee.guide.web/bldghist.numbers.html

"Recalculating the Infinite Corridor" reprinted from hacks.mit.edu/Hacks/by_year /1997/infinity_rods/

"Student Leaders at MIT Claim Harvard as Colony" reprinted from *The Journal of the Institute for Hacks, TomFoolery & Pranks at MIT.*

"Hacking by Mail" reprinted from *The Journal of the Institute for Hacks, TomFoolery & Pranks at MIT.*

"The Case of the Disappearing President's Office" reprinted from *Is This the Way to Baker House?*

"Door Man" reprinted from *The Journal of the Institute for Hacks, TomFoolery & Pranks at MIT.*

"The Great Breast of Knowledge" reprinted from *The Journal of the Institute for Hacks, TomFoolery & Pranks at MIT.*

"Where the Sun Shines, There Hack They" reprinted from *Is This the Way to Baker House?*

"Engineering in Action" reprinted from *Is This the Way to Baker House?*

Photo Credits

We have made every effort to secure permissions and credit information for all photographs used in this book.

Page	
2	Bettmann/CORBIS
3	Joe Dennehey, Boston Globe (top)
8–9	Brian Leibowitz
13	E. Robert Schildkraut
14	Donna Coveney, Tech Talk (top)
14	Marc PoKempner, Tech Talk (bottom)
15	Jon Williams (top)
18	Carl Bazil (top)
18	E. Robert Schildkraut (bottom)
20	Alan Devoe, Technique (top)
20	Donna Coveney, Tech Talk (bottom)
21	Terri Iuzzolino Matsakis (right)
22	Terri Iuzzolino Matsakis
23	Donna Coveney, MIT News Office
24–25	Terri Iuzzolino Matsakis
26	Erik Nygren
29	Brian Leibowitz
31	Bill Hoffman, Technique
32	Chun Lim Lau, Technique
33	Tien Nguyen (right)
35	Terri Iuzzolino Matsakis
38	Paula M. Lerner, Tech Talk
39	Simson Garfinkel, The Tech
40	Donald Davidoff, Technique
42–43	Terri Iuzzolino Matsakis
44–46	Erik Nygren
47	Andre DéHon
48	Terri Iuzzolino Matsakis
49	Andre DéHon (top)
49	Terri Iuzzolino Matsakis (bottom)
50	Andre DéHon
51	Eri Izawa/Michael J. Bauer
53	Terri Iuzzolino Matsakis
54	Brian Leibowitz
55	Erik Nygren
58	Simson Garfinkel
59	Terri Iuzzolino Matsakis
61	Marc Horowitz (top)
61	Donna Coveney, Tech Talk (bottom)
63	Brian Leibowitz
67	M. C. Escher's "Relativity" © 2002 Cordon Art B.V. – Baarn–Holland. All rights reserved. Bruner-Cott & Associates-Architects/D. deAngeli
68–69	Brian Leibowitz
70–71	Terri Iuzzolino Matsakis
72	Ron M. Hoffmann
77–79	Terri Iuzzolino Matsakis
83	Terri Iuzzolino Matsakis
86	David M. Watson
87	Jeff Thiemann
88	Larry-Stuart Deutsch
89	Terri Iuzzolino Matsakis
90	Carl Lacombe, Technique
91	Peter Buttner
92	Steve Slesinger (bottom)
94	Oren Levine, Technique

95	Brian Leibowitz
98	© Harold & Esther Edgerton Foundation, 2002, courtesy of Palm Press, Inc.
99	Brian Leibowitz (bottom)
100	The Tech
104	Brian Leibowitz
105–106	Terri Iuzzolino Matsakis
107	Donna Coveney, Tech Talk
109	Terri Iuzzolino Matsakis
110	Erik Nygren
111	Terri Iuzzolino Matsakis
116	Brian Leibowitz
121	Boston Herald
126–127	Heather Howard Chesnais
130	Donna Coveney, Tech Talk
131	Boston Globe (left), reproduced with permission of Boston Globe via Copyright Clearance Center (right)
132–133	Bob Brooks
134	Bob Brooks (top)
135	Bob Brooks
137	Terri Iuzzolino Matsakis
139	The Tech
141	Gene Dixon, Boston Herald American
142	Terri Iuzzolino Matsakis
143–144	Erik Nygren
157–158	Terri Iuzzolino Matsakis